KNOW THE HINDU MIND

KNOW THE HINDU MIND

V.T. Rajshekar

GYAN

ISBN : 978-81-212-1288-5

First Published, 2015

Published by

Gyan Publishing House
23, Main Ansari Road, Darya Ganj,
New Delhi- 110 002
Ph. : 2328 2060, 2326 1060
E-mail: books@gyanbooks.com

Printed at : Reliable Infomedia, New Delhi

Cataloging in Publication Data—DK
Courtesy: D.K. Agencies (P) Ltd. <docinfo@dkagencies.com>

Rajshekar Shetty, V. T., 1932- **author.**
Know the Hindu mind / V.T. Rajshekar.
pages cm
Reprint.
ISBN 9788121212885

1. Hinduism—Psychology. 2. Social conflict—India. 3. Hinduism and social problems. I. Title.

DDC 294.5019 23

Contents

FOREWORD FOR THE SECOND REVISED EDITION

As this is written India, which became "independent" in 1947, is 61 years old and China is two years younger. Yet our giant neighbour has overtaken us to become a world power.

The *Times of India* (Jan.14, 2008), which has emerged as the country's largest circulated English daily and the darling of its Brahminical ruling class, in a report to coincide with Prime Minister Manmohan Singh's visit to China said in a report headlined:

> "India (is) no position to strike (China): Unequal status will make it difficult for PM to call the shot".

Then it lists 12 items like GDP, forex reserves, population below 1 $ a day and 2$ a day, rice and wheat productivity, life expectancy, underweight children, infant mortality, maternal mortality, public health expenditure, telephones (million), internet users (million). In all the 12 items, India is beaten hollow. As of today China's economy is three times bigger than India's.

How did China gallop and India fall behind?

Our Brahminical rulers have a stock answer: "India is a democracy but China is communist".

China is a godless country but we have our 330 million gods, still larger number of godmen, our ancient "religion" of Hinduism with a treacherous value system. Why nobody saved us? Rather, they are the cause of our failure.

All rational minds admit this fact but the "Hindu India" will not because the "Hindu mind" is irrational and cannot think scientifically.

When we were young, like all other Hindus we too were living in the dungeon of Hinduism but by the time we became a graduate, we understood the dangers of Hinduism and got attracted to marxism. And rejected Hinduism. But within ten years we were convinced that Brahminism, which is parading as Hinduism, swallowed even marxism and killed its egalitarian spirit. Our book, *How Marx Failed in Hindu India* (1980), is the result of this awareness. Our marxist friends did not agree with our analysis and interpretation because they were Hindu first and marxist last. That is how marxism died young in Hindu India.

Then we went over to Ambedkarism which came as a refreshing force to liberate the country's oppressed millions — lowest of the low, being the Untouchables. Our study of Ambedkarism revealed that it is marxism plus something more. But in the last 30 years our experience is that Brahminism is creeping even into Ambedkarism. And that is how even Ambedkarism is struggling to survive.

There is not a single institution which has not been corrupted and co-opted by Brahminism. (Please note our criticism is against Brahminism and not against any individual Brahmin).

Our considered opinion (as the country is completing 61 years) is if India has to live Brahminism (Hinduism) has to die.

But what actually is happening is all those people who have the courage to speak out this supreme truth are gagged and suffocated and Hinduism, if it can be called a religion, is getting new life and new vigour even as the country is gradually sinking.

This is our sad verdict after spending over 50 years in daily paper journalism and later as Editor of the *Dalit Voice* for 27 years.

But no Hindu is realising that his Hinduism is causing India's slow death. If there is any Hindu who has the courage to say it, he is called mad. Call the dog mad and shoot.

India's parliament, the entire executive, judiciary headed by its Supreme Court, media, the whole academic world, all scientific institutions have simply collapsed and surrendered before the awful power of Brahminism. Original thinking is simply dead.

What is much more shocking is even non-Hindu liberating religions like Islam, Christianity and Sikhism have been throttled and made to live at the mercy of Hinduism. The leadership of all these three religions have been *hinduised* (meaning enslaved).

What about the country's Untouchables — a formidable 20% of the population — who under the revolutionary leadership of Dr. Babasaheb Ambedkar were told that "they are not Hindu and were never Hindu?" The Brahminical rulers under the leadership of M.K. Gandhi used the "Poona Pact" (1932) to subvert Dr. Ambedkar's demand for separate electorate and when the constitution was drafted in 1950-51 the Untouchables were brought under Hinduism and once for all imprisoned. The fate of the country's only revolutionary section, which alone had the capacity to revolt and kill Brahminism, was once for all sealed.

So this multi-ethnic country of hundreds of castes and communities — the world's second largest populated country after China — is finally drowned in the gutter of Hinduism and stinking.

So much so it is the Hindus, precisely the tiny 3% Brahmins, who rule this country and everybody else has to live under their mercy. And this Brahminical micro-minority ruling class in its bid to continue its rulership is dragging this ancient country down the precipice. What is shocking is even this slow death of India is completely hidden from the eyes of the drowning people by its Brahminical media. And the mass murder of its 1,115 million people is itself made painless under the powerful drug called Hinduism. It may look exaggerated but it is true. Believe me, even the very rulers, Brahmins, are not happy.

All over the world we have slavery but India is the one and the only country which has not only slaves but a set of wonderful slaves who actually enjoy their slavery. Have you heard of it anywhere in the world?

Over 60% of India's population is almost illiterate. India itself has turned out to be the world's largest country of illiterates. And Hinduism has further squeezed these illiterates by making them unthinking morons.

So much so thinking itself has stopped in India. Anybody thinking is frowned at and if he or she persists in thinking the person is called mad. Call the dog mad and shoot.

Even a rare intellectual giant like Dr. Babasaheb Ambedkar, who worked and died for the liberation of the entire oppressed masses of India, is hated by the Hindus.

Even after decades of his death the Brahminical rulers of India have no heart to admit his greatness. How can a superman take birth outside the heaven-born *Bhoodevatas*? This is their dilemma.

What then is wrong with Hinduism? People all over the world except communist societies believe in god. Muslims, Christians, Sikhs, Jews all have their god and religion. All religionists all over the world are ready to face an inquiry on their god and religion. But the Hindu is not because his life (even after death) is regulated by his religion at every moment.

Will the Hindu accept the test of **justice** and the test of **utility** to judge the philosophy of Hinduism? First the test of justice which is another name for liberty, equality, fraternity. The caste system —with its ascending order of reverence and descending degree of contempt —seriously violates the very principle of equality as it assigns gradation and rank to each caste which in other words means inequality. That means Hinduism does not (never, ever) recognise equality. Inequality is the guiding principle of caste system. Somebody is above you and somebody is below you. The Untouchables being the lowest of the low are the worst hated under this system.

Those above gets the satisfaction and the pride that somebody is below them and are lording over them. But they don't know that some fellows sitting above their heads are shitting and pissing. But they will not mind it as long as they have the right to shit and piss on somebody else's head. This is caste system — unique to Hindu India— and unless it is set on fire Hindus will continue to be sick — but neither living nor dead. This is the state of India today. But the Hindus are not realising it.

Having been fed up with marxism, which Brahminism swallowed, we turned to Ambedkarism (though we are not born Untouchable) which our study revealed as the most revolutionary philosophy assuring revolution in Hindu India. That is how we started the *Dalit Voice* to attack and destroy the very foundations of Brahminism by whipping up the slaves (Dalits) and rousing them to action. The problem of India is not poverty (as made out by our rulers) but the graded inequality and exploitation under the Brahminical caste system.

No doubt we have succeeded to a great extent but the Brahmins with their mass media in their hands are more influential to undo whatever we can do through our tiny *Dalit Voice* in English though we had six language editions headed by a Hindi edition published from Delhi.

As the country grew up and more and more Dalits got educated and got jobs through reservation (the total achievement through reservation is only 5%), the Brahminical rulers caught hold of the "educated", employed Dalits and brain-washed them in Brahminical thinking and a substantial section of Dalits once again fell into the Brahminical trap and became better slaves of Hindus. It is the educated and employed Dalits (who are not even 5% of the Dalit population) instead of becoming the vanguard of the Dalit revolutionaries they became pawns in the Brahminical chess board and got alienated from the 95% of the uneducated, village-dwelling dirt poor Dalits.

Once again the Brahminical counter-revolution checkmated the revolution by *Hinduising* the non-Hindu (educated) Dalits.

Muslims were the other revolutionary group (15%) which had the capacity, courage and a formidable religious weapon. But here again the Brahminical counter-revolution succeeded by dividing India's Muslim society. At least 5% of the country's Muslims are English-educated and fairly rich. But it is this Muslim "leadership" that has been *hinduised* and enslaved. The rest of the Muslims remain dirt poor, in urban slums, unemployed and permanently facing Hindu police atrocities in hundreds of anti-Muslim riots and dubbed terrorists. Muslims form the single largest population today in Indian jails.

With Dalits and Muslims, the two most revolutionary sections, neutralised where is the chance for any revolution?

Of course the naxalite (maoist) problem has become more serious compared to "terrorism" (read Muslim) but the Brahminical leadership is not worried about naxalism because its leadership is in their hands and those who die facing police bullets are the country's Dalits, Tribals or Backward Castes — all enemies of rulers. The police who die out of naxal violence are again the same stuff. That is how the Hindu rulers of India are not as much perturbed over naxal violence as terrorist (Muslim) violence.

With Dalit (Ambedkarite) revolution ruled out, Muslim terrorism mercilessly suppressed, naxalite *natak* companies managed, the Brahminical counter-revolution today faces no opposition.

The country, as a consequence, is fast going downhill under the Brahminical counter-revolution which has been going on since centuries.

This book attempts to place before our readers a picture of this on-going Brahminical counter-revolution.

Place: Bangalore

Date: August 1, 2008

V.T. Rajshekar

FOREWORD FOR THE FIRST EDITION

This book is going to press at a time when the country is in the midst of a mad, mad general election (1989) which gives us enough opportunity to understand the working of the "Hindu mind". We are consciously using the word "Hindu" because we have no other word that can be so easily understood. By "Hindu" or the Brahminical Social Order (BSO) we mean India's micro-minority upper castes (Aryans), just about 15% of the country's population. They only are the "Hindu". The rest are not Hindu. What are called Scheduled Castes, the Scheduled Tribes in the Constitution of India are the country's indigenous population and hence pre-Aryan. They are not Hindu and were never Hindu. Together they (SC/ST) make up a population of 20%+10%=30%. The Other Backward Castes (OBCs) listed by the Mandal Commission Report are Dravidians and hence they are also country's indigenous population. OBCs are neither *shudras* nor Hindu as many OBCs themselves believe.

Only the four *varnas* come under the *chaturvarna*. They are the Brahmin, Kshatriya, Vaishya and the *shudra*. If the OBCs are *shudra*, they automatically become Hindu. But the OBCs are also Untouchables in varying degrees.

So, the OBCs are neither *shudra* nor Hindu and their population is an estimated at 35% or so. That means (20+10+35) a total of 65% of India's population is not "Hindu".

We have repeated this sociological fact and historical truth in many of our speeches and writings and published it in many issues of the *Dalit Voice* and also our books. To this day no Hindu "social scientist" has challenged either our facts or figures.

The Muslims (15%), Christians (2.5%) and Sikhs (2.5%), a total of about 20%, are any way not "Hindu". So, the 65% SC/ST/BCs and 20% "religious minorities" make up a total of 85%.

When the Hindus claim that the Hindus constitute an "overwhelming majority of India comprising 85% of its population", they are manufacturing statistics or lies by including the 65% of the indigenous non-Hindu population with their micro-minority 15% population. For purposes of job reservations, for sharing the human rights enjoyed by Hindus, SC/ST/BCs do not become Hindu but outsiders. When the SC/ST/BCs seek admission into their temples, they are kicked, killed, burnt, raped and their little properties destroyed. They become "Hindu" only during elections, census operations and during anti-Muslim or Sikh riots. After these three limited purposes are over, these "Hindus" are discarded and treated as outsiders or hostile forces. This in brief is the story of the "Hindu love" for those fondly called "Hindu".

This Hindu discrimination against SC/ST/BCs and Muslims/ Christians/Sikhs has led to the partition of India (1947)and later widespread unrest and consequent violence endangering the very unity and integrity of the country of which we Dalits, its real owners, are very much worried. Because every division of India has been reducing our population making us more and more vulnerable to the Aryan aggression on Indian culture.

This book is intended as a humble attempt at analysing the causes of this unrest and violence. The principal cause is the working of this enigmatic "Hindu mind". The world outside is simply perplexed by this "Hindu mind". Because without knowing the "Hindu mind" and making a study of it, none can understand this "Hindu mind".

We would have been happy if such a working of the "Hindu mind" had brought peace, prosperity, happiness and security at least to the Hindus, the rulers. But as per their own admission, they are miserable. They say they feel threatened every minute.

Rulers feeling threatened? Heard of it anywhere? Since the country's entire wealth is concentrated in their hands, they are feeling insecure and hence raising the height of their compound walls and many of them are employing private armed guards. In Delhi, the country's capital, the rulers are living a miserable life as virtual prisoners barricated by armed security guards.

Nothing that is managed by them for their own pleasure and pomp is working satisfactorily. The Indian Airlines, the domestic carrier, is in a mess. The cities where the rulers live have turned into vast slums. One Hindu is complaining against the other Hindu about corruption and corruption is eating them wholesale. Scientific and technological institutions have broken down, abounding in frauds. Educational institutions have come to a standstill. Every section of the ruling class is on strike at one or other place or time complaining against another section of that class. Ecology has collapsed. Within 40 years of the "Hindu rule", India has been plundered, pillaged and pulped.

All this is the result of this diabolic "Hindu mind", the working of which we are honestly not able to understand. Not only it has enslaved the 85% of non-Hindus but pushed the Hindus themselves to utter frustration. The Hindus themselves are miserable, mentally sick and their misery is causing anxiety. All because of the working of this "Hindu mind".

We did not cause their mental sickness. They are the cause of their own madness. The latest being the defeat for Hindus on the Ram Janambhoomi. They demolished the Babri Masjid but failed to build the temple of their favourite god, Ram. They wanted to scrap the existing parliamentary democracy and establish a presidential system of government. In this also they failed. Everywhere they are meeting with defeat and as days pass they are reaching desperation and a dead-end. A careful reading of their own Hindu "national press" gives us ample clues to their panicked state of mind.

Had this sickness afflicted only them, it would have been a worry of the mere 15% rulers — though as the real owners of the country we want everybody to be healthy for the sake of the country's happiness. But this sick "Hindu mind" is not only killing itself but this sickness is spreading unrest and violence to the rest of India. This is our real worry.

What is the remedy for this mental sickness? People with unsound mind are called insane and are taken to a psychiatrist. And if necessary they have to be admitted to a mental hospital. Will the "Hindu mind" get itself admitted to a mental hospital?

We have little hope of the Hindus realising their mistake. This is because of the Hindu dictum that the "Hindu" commits no mistake. His logic is that he alone is right and the whole world is wrong. He says he has nothing to learn or unlearn. The problem with the Hindus is that they don't know that they are mentally unsound. The stage of consulting a doctor and getting the disease diagnosed comes only when the patient realises that he is ill and wants to get himself cured. This hope is not there as the Hindu is not only not aware of his sickness but thinks that he is the world's most healthy, wealthy and wise man. That is why the Hindu is hated in Nepal, Pakistan, Bangladesh, distant Fiji and even in African countries. Wherever a Hindu goes, he creates hatred.

So, in the interest of saving our country's unity and integrity, it is the duty of the real owners of the land — the SC/ST/BCs and their co-sufferers, Muslims/Christians/Sikhs — to realise the predicament of the Hindus, their helplessness and save them by getting the sick "Hindu mind" admitted to the mental asylum.

Bangalore, India

V.T. Rajshekar

Nov.22, 1989.

----

1 – Introduction

A Hindu terrorist organisation in Bangalore once (1989) raised a big controversy on the abattoir (a modern slaughter house proposed by the Karnataka Govt. in Bangalore). On this, I don't know whether to laugh or to weep. India's upper caste rulers have mastered the art of raising controversies on simple non-issues like this to divert the attention of the persecuted people from burning issues.

Ever since India got "independence" (1947) they have been raising one "controversy" or the other so that the slaves are made to quarrel between themselves on non-issues. Silly and stupid controversies are deliberately raised with the help of their own Brahminical monopoly media to divert the mind of the slaves from grave issues like denial of human rights, food, clothing, shelter, health and educational facilities. If these people, denied their human rights, are allowed to think of their deprivation, they will certainly explode. And any explosion on human rights issues will affect the properties and privileges of the ruling class. Hence the rulers go on manufacturing non-issues like this silly controversy on abattoir. This is the secret behind the "abattoir controversy".

To the upper caste rulers such "controversies" provide an opportunity to become heroes out of zeroes. And to some others, it provides an entertainment at the cost of our pain.

However, these "controversies" are confined only to the upper castes (*savarnas*/Hindus/Aryans) who are not even 15% of India's 1,100 million population. India's newspaper-reading population is itself less than 10%. Fortunately, the rest of the population is untouched by these silly "controversies". But by confusing the top 15% of the population, these Hindus create one havoc after another and thereby they are able to destroy the time and energies of the people. This typical Hindu game is reduced to a fine art and to understand this fine art, it is necessary that we should first make a study of the "Hindu mind".

The ruling class is deliberately creating these controversies to fool our innocent people and thereby enslave them. Alright? So the conspiracy behind this game is to frighten and fool us. And when we get confused, it is easier to enslave us. The "abattoir controversy" that once raged in Bangalore was one such.

Dalit-Muslim unity

But please note that these Hindu rulers by creating this controversy have also done us some good. The very slaves whom the Hindus wanted to keep divided — mainly the Dalits and Muslims — got united on this issue. The "abattoir controversy" gave a big boost to the badly-needed Dalit-Muslim unity. The Hindus while opposing the abattoir were mainly interested in hurting the Muslims who as butchers were mainly engaged in the animal slaughter work. So they tried to engineer this "abattoir controversy" to hit the Muslim stomach. But the affected poor Muslims approached the Dalit Sangharsha Samiti whose Dalit followers are mainly beef-eaters.

The Hindus while trying to enslave us do not know they are unconsciously digging their own grave. So on behalf of the SC/ST/BCs and Muslim/Christians, I thank the Hindus of Bangalore for creating such a "crisis" and forcing the Dalit/Muslim/Christian unity: the unity of sufferers and co-sufferers.

The Hindus must create more such "controversies" so that the slaves can identify their enemy and get united to throw away their slavery.

Pakistan & Khalistan

What are the different mind-manipulating tricks these Hindus — killers of M.K. Gandhi — play to fool the gullible masses and keep them divided and thereby enslave them? The "abattoir controversy" is not merely an attack on the Muslim, using the cow slaughter issue as a stick to beat them, but more a sort of cultural aggression to silence and suppress the original inhabitants of India. (V.T. Rajshekar, *Aggression on Indian Culture*, Dalit Sahitya Akademy, 1988).

The Hindus have thus provided us with a very wonderful opportunity. Therefore, I want to make the following points and I request the Hindus to commit more such aggressions which in turn will help us correct our mistakes and promote the unity and integrity of India.

If the Hindus continue with such silly, stupid "controversies" on non-issues like the abattoir, they will be only promoting the disunity and disintegration of India. In the past, every act of dismembering the country was done by these very Hindus. It is these very Hindus who were responsible for driving out a section of the Muslims to form Pakistan. It was these very same Hindus who persecuted the Sikhs and forced them to seek Khalistan.

Electric crematorium

Hence it is necessary that we have a peep into the working of this "Hindu mind", this perverted mind. (*Dalit Voice* Editorial, Jan.1, 1989: *"Twist in the Hindu mind"*).

When I was in the *Indian Express* (before 1980), the Karnataka Govt. decided to start an electric crematorium in Bangalore. At that time also, these very same sick minds raised a big "controversy". They opposed the electric crematorium saying that it was against their (Hindu) *dharma*. It is easy for them to raise any "controversy" because the entire media is in their pocket and the *chaddi* (*khaki* half pant) boys going by the name of "journalists" can convert a donkey into a race horse overnight. So hell was let lose on the crematorium controversy.

But today you go to the Wilson Garden or Harischandra Ghat crematorium (Bangalore), you will find these very Hindus standing in queue to cremate their dead.

The point is the Hindus oppose every scientific and technological progress and build up "public opinion' against using scientific tools so that the masses remain backward and hence in poverty. At the same time, they will be the first people to make full advantage of science and technology and harness it to their best advantage.

This is what I call as the "Hindu mind".

Computers

Then came the computer controversy. Do you remember those days? India's "sacred thread marxists" raised a big furore against the introduction of computers. They said computers would result in large-scale unemployment. A countrywide agitation was launched. For about one year upper caste-led trade unions went on a rampage against computers. Communist-led trade unions like AITUC, CITU etc. engineered strikes in LIC, banks, and all over. They even ransacked and burnt some computers.

Today, what is the position? You will see the same "sacred thread" people overnight turning into computer kids monopolising the entire computer technology — since renamed Information Technology (IT). Not only they have taken over the computers but they are using these very computers against us — to oppress us.

As the upper castes own the media, they can convert a donkey into a race horse and a race horse into a bloody ass. They converted Prime Minister Rajiv Gandhi into "Mr. Clean". And the very same "Mr. Clean" was overnight dubbed "Mr. Dirtiest" with Bofors and Fairfax. Because the press is in their hands. And thereby they can "manufacture" any public opinion.

Earlier, they "managed" the SC/ST/BCs and Muslim/Christian/Sikhs to develop a prejudice against computers and when that field became free, the cross-threads went and grabbed it. That is why we should make a study of this "Hindu mind". Today, the entire computer technology (IT) is an upper caste monopoly.

Our Hindu rulers have perfected this ingenious technic of exploitation, this mind-manipulation game. Unless we make a study of this technic, we cannot fight the Hindus. None in the whole world has perfected such a mind-manipulating technic in which our upper castes are the supreme masters.

Mother tongue mania

Here is a more effective example to prove my point: this English language. The rulers simply made us believe that English is a "foreign language". They asked the SC/ST/BCs to read Kannada, eat Kannada, sleep in Kannada and die in Kannada. (*Dalit Voice,* Aug.16, 1988: *"Right to study English language denied to SC/ST/BCs & minorities; Upper caste rulers imposing linguistic imperialism"*).

A mad love for Kannada and a blind hatred for English has been created. (This is the case in every state of India). And all of us are made to blindly believe that Kannada is our "mother", our life breath and English is our deadly poison. English is the root cause of our poverty, prejudice, enslavement. And every ill of the country is attributed to English. They said English, the language of the British rulers, was used to rule us for 200 years and keep India as a slave country. We all believed it blindly. Having been made bloody fools, we blindly believed this false propaganda as a gospel truth. And we discarded English (the world's only international language) and even started hating it. This mad mother tongue mania they created in us made our people to die as clerks and peons while the Brahmin lorded over the land like a colossus.

Language of dogs

Anybody speaking in favour of English is dubbed anti-national. By resorting to this mind-manipulating fine art, they successfully denied the knowledge of English to over 95% of India's population. But the cross-threads were the first to quietly master the English language which proved to be the gateway to knowledge. The slaves were made to develop hatred against English and they voluntarily left the English language to the upper castes who mastered and used the very same English language to further enslave us.

That is why I say: study this ingenious "Hindu mind".

So much so, after 61 years of "independence", English has become the language of the rulers. And the slaves are told to be satisfied with the Indian languages. Upper caste children go to "private" schools, master English, become rulers and our children go to "public" schools and become slaves taking a false pride in our "mother tongue" and thereby remain clerks and peons.

This is the genius of the "Hindu mind". Let anything happen to the country and its people but we must prosper at any cost. This is the genius of the "Hindu mind". Heard of it anywhere in the world?

Karnataka once had a Brahmin Chief Minister, Ramakrishna Hegde. His children could hardly speak Kannada. But Hegde was a bitter opponent of English in public to keep our people in perpetual darkness. In Jayanagar, Indiranagar, Palace Orchards, in all such fashionable localities, upper castes speak even to their dogs in English. I was in a Brahmin house and was surprised to find the kids in his house speaking to their dog in English. When I asked the kids why they were not speaking in Kannada to their dog, they said: "Uncle, our dog doesn't know *Canada*". Even this word Kannada, their own mother tongue, they cannot pronounce properly.

Sanskrit role

In the United States, the Whites are the rulers. They are the rulers and Blacks are slaves. But the White rulers have not denied the knowledge of English to the Blacks. So also in the Apartheid days of South Africa. Both the Whites and the Blacks spoke only English. But India is the one and only country where even a language is used to enslave its people. Earlier, these cross-threads used Sanskrit to enslave the *shudras* and today they are using English to enslave us.

That is why I say you must study the "Hindu mind".

Kannada (or Hindi) for the slaves and English for the rulers. This is the Hindu technic of enslaving people. That is why even after 60 years of "independence", the English literacy in India is less than 5% of the population. Any attempt to teach English from the primary class is stubbornly resisted on all sorts of flimsy grounds. But all the critics of English send their children only to English schools. The cross-thread technique is so effective and deadly that if we advocate English, our own Dalit boys are made to pounce on us for speaking against their mother (tongue).

Temple entry stunts

Upper castes (Hindus) are the very people who oppose the *Harijan* entry into temples. In different parts of India, Untouchables entering temples are beaten up and insulted. But at the same time these are the very people who are leading *Harijans* into temples. Both are done by the same people. "Socialist Brahmins" like M.K. Gandhi, Agnivesh "lead" *Harijans* into temples and "Sacred Brahmins" like Puri Swami etc, get our people beaten up inside the temples. What happened at the Nathadwara temple in Rajasthan was a Hindu conspiracy to glorify "Socialist Brahmins" leading *Harijans* into the temple and the "Sacred Brahmins" beating up our people. In the process the Brahmin becomes the hero at our cost. The Brahmins become heroes but our people remain where they are. Have you ever heard of such an indigenous technique?

Gandhi's crooked mind

This could only be the work of a devilish "Hindu mind".

What is the intention behind these temple entry stunts? If they lead the *Harijans* into temples, those "leading' it — namely the "gandhians" become heroes and those *Harijans* who enter the temple become better slaves. So this temple entry is a double-edged sword. It cuts both ways. Dr. Babasaheb Ambedkar had strictly opposed and criticised temple entry. Why should we go to a place which is not only not ours but belongs to our enemy?

That is why you should make a study of the "Hindu mind".

Harijans (the hated name given by Gandhi) are not Hindu and were never Hindu. They have nothing to do with Hindu temples. They are not interested in entering the Hindu temples. But Gandhi by creating a desire in the hearts of *Harijans* to enter Hindu temple, did the greatest damage to Untouchables. Because it is such temple-entry stunts of Gandhi that made the Untouchables **think** they are Hindu. And once they **think** they are Hindu, they can be easily annexed to the Hindu fold and given the status of a class below the *shudras*.

If Gandhi had not appeared on the Indian scene, the Untouchables of India under the leadership of Dr. Babasaheb Ambedkar would have established their separate identity through "separate electorate" (against which Gandhi went on a fast) and later enmasse would have become Budhists. It was Gandhi who was primarily responsible for the present conditions of Untouchables hovering between life and death.

Largest slave country in the world

It is again this crooked "Hindu mind" that worked. Gandhi might have succeeded in his mission of blocking the liberation of Untouchables and thereby he might have secured to the Hindus the services of unpaid bonded slaves. But at what cost? Thereby Gandhi converted India into the single largest slave country in the world. This is the result of the queer "Hindu mind".

People talk of the nazis of Germany and their "holocaust".

Muslims talk about the zionists and say these two peoples have perfected a perfect technique of persecution. But I say that India's Brahminical technique of enslavement has no parallel in the whole world.

It is said the German nazis have put Jews into gas chamber. The exaggerated version of "holocaust" speak of millions of Jews being killed like this. The difference between the nazi technique and the Hindu technique is the former threatened violence against Jews and honestly used violence to kill Jews. But in "Hindu India" very, very rarely violence is used against SC/ST/BCs. They used only "non-violence". Because they did not want to kill us. Killing us would deprive them of their free slaves. Nobody kills his slave. Because he needs the slave. So the Hindu wanted the slave. Gandhi is hailed as the "Apostle of non-violence" for his ingenious technique of enslaving SC/ST/BCs without using violence.

If anybody wants to test my claims, please read Chanakya's *Arthasastra* (Shama Sastry, Padma Printers, Mysore, 1988). Mrs. Indira Gandhi, India's most famous Brahminical ruler, experimented the *Arthasastra* in her "Blue Star Operation" (1984).

Beef tallow business

The whole thing is intended to confuse us. Recollect the famous "Beef tallow controversy" that went on for six months. Do you know who was finally arrested? The "*Shudda Vanaspati*" company owner — a Marwari Jain from Delhi. This Bania must have made tons of money by exporting beef tallow. And all those fellows who were in the forefront of the beef tallow agitations were mostly Jains and the *chaddi* boys. The "beef tallow controversy" was manufactured to terrorise the Muslims and to poison the minds of non-Muslims against Muslims, saying that the Muslims kill the "mother cow" and the beef fat is mixed in vegetable ghee or *vanaspati* to prepare eatables. The whole idea was to portray the Muslims as monsters. Finally, after months of allegations which got full publicity in the Brahminical media, the culprit was arrested. Jains claim to be "pure vegetarians" but they would not mind provoking anti-Muslim violence.

Even the "abattoir controversy" in Bangalore was led by a Marwadi Jain — aided and abetted by the *chaddi* boys. The game plan was to frighten the Muslims and instigate the Dalits against them. And when the two brothers fight, it is these upper castes — Marwadis, the cross-threads and the Banias etc. — who reap the harvest.

That is why I want you to make a study of this "Hindu mind".

Who is anti-national?

The upper castes (Hindus) are the people who call everybody else anti-national, seditious, terrorists etc. They frighten us daily with the two magic *mantra* of "unity" and "integrity"? But do you know that all those people who were arrested and jailed for anti-national activities were all upper castes? They were arrested for spying for foreign countries and for stealing cabinet secrets. Have you forgotten the case of Kumar Narayan (Iyer). Either in the "Bofors" or "Fairfax" — all those who took the bribes were upper castes. Who is Win Chadda? Our people have never been accused of anti-national activities. The Kudal Commission has indicted the country's "Gandhians", most of them Brahmins, for accepting foreign funds and using that funds for anti-national activities. (*Dalit Voice*, Editorial Sept.1, 1989: "*Nazis in the garb of Gandhians*"). Take the case of Harshad Mehta who destabilised the entire economy of the country during P.V. Narasimha Rao's prime ministership. He was a Gujarati Jain Bania.

The upper castes speak of "unity and integrity" but they are the very people who destroy the unity and integrity of India.

Merit & caste

They say that "caste criterion" to determine backwardness must go. They want "backwardness" to be determined only on the basis of "poverty" — what they call as 'economic criterion". But they are the very people who promote caste by organising Brahmin conferences. These cross-threads want "poverty yardstick" and not caste-based job reservations. Every *jati* among Brahmins is having its own association and regular meetings are held and reported in the media. But once they come out of the meetings, these very Brahmins criticise caste-based reservations, caste-based movements. They have one rule for themselves and one for others.

But the same people want the post of temple priests should be a caste-based reservation, exclusively reserved for Brahmins. Why they are opposing "merit-based" appointments to the posts of temple-priests? The Tamil Nadu Govt. had passed a legislation to train temple priests (*archakas*) from all castes on the basis of "merit" but the Brahmins challenged it and the Brahminical Supreme Court obliged them. Why they sing two different tunes?

We have hundreds of reported cases of upper castes securing false caste certificates and enjoying SC/ST reservations — even while opposing reservations. Quite a number of them were convicted for such offences.

To understand such a fantastic twisted mind you must first make a study of the "Hindu mind".

Prani Daya

During the "abattoir controversy" in Bangalore, they were speaking of *Prani Daya* (kindness to animals) but why can't the same people have some kindness for human beings (*Manushya Daya*)? These people have formed societies "to prevent cruelty to animals", birds, insects, stones, trees, water, air, environment. All sorts of "societies" are formed to prevent "cruelty" but to this day we have not come across one single "society to prevent cruelty to human beings".

In Delhi, monkey menace is a common feature. These forest-dwelling creatures have invaded the capital city because the trees in the Himalayan forests have all disappeared and to fill their stomach they descend on Delhi and lay siege even on the central secretariat and many union ministry buildings. But we have a strange creature in Delhi called Menaka Gandhi, a darling of the Hindu terrorist party. She won't allow anybody to touch the monkeys even if they enter your office and bite you. Even the courts dare not touch this Menaka Memsaheb. Such is the "Hindu power" in this country.

Finally after the rulers sitting inside these central govt. offices became helpless, they decided to catch these monkeys and take them back to the forests — spending any amount of money. But the "Hindu heart" will not tolerate the death of a monkey. Because the monkey is god Hanuman to these Hindus. Every dangerous creature including the serpents are gods to these people.

The milk of human kindness is over-flowing in their breasts. They "love" anything and everything except the human beings. I have seen rich, fat upper castes bringing bagful of grains and throwing it to birds at the India Gate, New Delhi. I have seen them feeding rats and bandicoots. I have seen them feeding fish. I have seen them feeding monkeys, serpents and all sorts of dangerous creatures. But I have never seen them lavishing this kindness on any human being.

When I asked them why they can't be equally kind to human beings and feed a starving child, the reply is:

"The child is starving because of the sin committed in its previous birth. It is the *karma* (destiny) which can't be changed. It has to suffer. That is why it is starving".

A very beautiful Hindu logic which has kept a third of the country below the poverty line, at the starvation level.

You will know their psychology only if you study the "Hindu mind".

Vegetarianism

Do you know why these Hindus speak of vegetarianism and glorify vegetarianism? This is to see that you (non-vegetarians) develop a contempt and hatred for your own food and hate what you eat. Once you give up eating meat, you will slowly become weak and you are deprived of the little animal protein. When you are mentally enslaved and physically enfeebled, you will surrender on your own.

This can only be the genious of the "Hindu mind".

They are the people who are destroying our trees. The entire forest wealth of India was destroyed by this ruling class. SC/ST/BCs and minorities are busy growing trees but it is these upper castes who are destroying the trees.

Chipko & Apiko

It is their own man (Sunderlal Bahuguna) who started the "Chipko movement" and became "famous". And another person of the same clan started the "Appiko movement" in Karnataka. Have you heard of these stunts? Sunderlal Bahuguna "fell in love with trees" and wide publicity the Brahmin media gave him for "going to forests and embracing trees". Why can't he for a change embrace a human being? He was given national and international awards to frighten us.

Did we not say they can convert a dirty donkey into a Derby horse?

These Hindus have formed "tree-lovers club", "animal-lovers club", "water-lovers club", "stone-lovers club", "insect-lovers club", "bird-lovers club" and "serpent-lovers club".

But to this day, they have not formed a single "human-lovers club".

Narmada Valley Project

"Environment", "ecology" has become a big business with the Hindus. This is their latest fad. So much so in *Dalit Voice,* we had published an article: "Beware of environmentalists". It is a pure and simple upper caste game to perpetuate the Hindu hegemony at the cost of the SC/ST/BCs. The most famous phantom created by the environmentalists is Medha Patkar.

That is why you must make a study of this quixotic "Hindu mind".

The Narmada Valley project is supposed to be the biggest river valley project in the whole country affecting three states of Gujarat, Madhya Pradesh and Maharashtra. Thousands of

Adivasis (tribals) are being uprooted and bundled out of their hearths and homes, their trees destroyed — so that the rivers are dammed and the fields of upper castes (mostly Patels) in Gujarat are made more fertile. The person heading the project in Gujarat was Sanat Mehta, a Gujarati Brahmin, and the entire upper castes of Gujarat and other two states are all agog about the coming boon from the Narmada. Because the Narmada Project serves two purposes: it enriches the upper castes and drives out the Adivasis from their homelands so that they can be *hinduised* (enslaved) and made to live as paupers and prostitutes. This is the grand upper caste design behind all river valley projects and after having tasted the double benefit of it, they want to push through the project for which the World Bank itself is giving the money. This is another advantage.

Lo & behold

Who is opposing the Narmada? Their own *jatwalas*, the Sunderlal Bahugunas, the Baba Amtes and the Medha Patkars. This is the beauty. Those wanting the Narmada Project are also upper castes and those opposing it are also the same set of people. Whichever party wins, the ultimate beneficiaries are only the upper castes. During the day, the two fight like cats and dogs but in the night they dine together and sleep together because they are all cousins and blood brothers. But the Chipko, Appiko and Narmada drama are all enacted to fool us. That is all. And they have their cousins in the media to conduct this puppet show. In the process, the Bahugunas, the Amtes, the Medha Patkars and such bogus people get international awards and rewards but the Adivasis will be left high and dry. This is the whole game of our so-called environmentalists who have become the latest menace to our society. The whole game of these environmentalists is to confuse the SC/ST/BCs and further pauperise them. Simple.

The entire forest wealth of India is virtually looted and destroyed by the cousins of these Amtes and Tamtes. Even the mighty Himalayas are not spared in their tree-felling madness. But these Bahugunas and Shivaram Karanths (since dead) go on getting publicity and all sorts of awards and rewards, even as their *jatwalas* are recklessly felling the trees and eating up the forest.

Such a contradiction can exist only in India — made possible only because of this amazing "Hindu mind".

Bogus scientists

Bangalore is said to be the "seat" of the country's premier scientific institutions. Indian Institute of Science, National Aeronautical Laboratory, Raman Institute, DRDO, GTRE, ISRO. Most of our "top scientists" live here.. Being scientists, they all must know that abattoir is a must for a growing city. But no scientist protested against this unscientific controversy. Because those agitating against the abattoir as well as these "scientists" belong to the same *jati*. They are all cousins. All these top "scientists" — ABCD Raos, BCG Raos, XYZ Raos, You R Raos, as well as Useless Rao, DDT Raos and the 420 Raos —know that abattoir is the most scientific method of slaughtering animals. But they will not say it in public. Why? Because the Hindus opposing the abattoir and the cross-thread scientists are all blood brothers. They are all bound by the same "sacred thread".

Same is the case with our "sacred-thread marxists".

In the marxist stronghold of Kerala, the Ayyappa temple at Sabarimala that attracts millions is flourishing with the full blessing of these red-hot marxists. If you question the marxists why they are allowing such a blatantly discriminatory practice of not allowing women to enter this temple, the reply is the marxists cannot interfere with the "faith" of the people. Can a "faith" which promotes superstition, discrimination against women, reckless plunder by a particular caste (Brahmins) be allowed in the name of faith? Sabarimala temple is hardly frequented by the Brahmins. But as its controllers they are exploiting it as a means to keep the Dalits and other "low castes", who rush there like flies and fall dead, as their perpetual slaves. The marxists of India are refusing to interfere in the Sabarimala affairs because it is used as instrument of Hindu oppression for which the marxists have their full blessings. E.M.S. Namboodaripad, Kerala's "Modern Shankara" killed the revolutionary fervour of the Backward Caste Ezhavas and Dalits by using marxism.

The wonder of India is our "marxists", Hindu terrorists, gandhians, and "scientists" are all bound by the same "sacred thread". Blood is thicker than water. To the upper castes their *jati* is above the society. They think they can prosper only if the society's prosperity is checked. It is this hatred in the Hindu heart that has made India what it is today.

Hypocrites

A relative living in Indiranagar (Bangalore) was telling me that whenever he went to the market in the mornings to get meat, he invariably found one or other cross-thread neighbour coming out with a bag. Even without his asking, the friend used to say that he (friend) came there to buy meat for his dog. Their guilty conscience made them speak at least half-truth. All these cross-threads eat meat secretly but want to put the blame on their poor dog. This is the typical "Hindu mind". A mind without heart.

Beef-eating Aryans

If it was meant for their dogs, they should take mainly bones. Why they take only the meat? Hypocrites. Nay. Traitors. They say one thing but do the exact opposite.

This is the result of the paranoid "Hindu mind".

The upper castes want to impress the outside world that they are "pure vegetarians" and that only vegetarian food is good for health. But the fish and meat prices have gone up because these grass-eaters have taken to meat. At least, we non-vegetarians are choosy in what meat we eat. But these grass-eaters once they start eating meat, they will eat even human flesh. Yes, their behaviour proves they are man-eaters.

Hinduism & Communism

Yet another twist in this "Hindu mind": Hinduism with its caste system is noted for its ascending order of reverence and descending degree of contempt. Hinduism does not believe in socialism, secularism and democracy. Nor does it believe in tolerance, equality, fraternity. Socialism and Hinduism simply cannot co-exist.

A Hindu terrorist party philosopher, M.S. Golwalkar, has listed in his party Bible, *Bunch of Thoughts* (Rashtrotthana Prakashana, Kempegowda Nagar, Bangalore - 560 019, 1980 pp.690), two internal and one external enemies for Hindus. The first two are Muslims and Christians. The external enemy is communism.

Golwalkar has also made it clear that Hindus are dead opposed to communism.

But who is heading all the "communist" parties in India— CPI, CPM and even naxalite (maoist) parties? They are all mostly Brahmins or some other upper castes. I have pointed out this as the major cause for failure of marxism in India today, (V.T. Rajshekar: *How Marx Failed in Hindu India?*, DSA-1989).

Marxism in India has been swallowed and digested by the Brahmins. In fact, marxism is being used by them to fight the non-Aryan people of India.

All-over India our people are today pitted more against "marxists" than against Hindu terrorists. In other words, many *chaddi* boys are turning to marxism to save their Hinduism. In Maharashtra, a Brahmin started a party after visiting the then Soviet Russia and impressed by the Soviet experiments at "controlling" the Muslims there. His theory ("Practical Socialism") is that in India only marxism can castrate the Muslims. Can you think of a more wonderful "Hindu mind" than this? In Bengal and Kerala, where the marxists have been in power for long, its main victims are Dalits, Backward Castes and Muslims who constitute the big majority. They vote for the marxists but the marxists keep them only as slaves. Marxism lost its appeal to the toiling masses only because it proved to be yet another instrument for the Brahmin to exploit our people.

Regional big bully

These Hindu rulers speak of peace, non-violence but practice the worst kind of violence on the non-Hindu population of India. They are also trying to impose their hegemony on the smaller countries surrounding India — Lanka, Pakistan, Nepal, Bangladesh, Maldives, Burma etc. So much so, India has come to be called the "regional big bully". Lanka is the most famous example. The burning hatred in the Hindu heart is the cause of this widespread unrest and the consequent violence.

China, which is fast coming up as a world power, became independent two years after India. Yet, it soon became the best friend of all its neighbours. Today all the neighbours of India hate India but love China. Even the world's only "Hindu nation", Nepal, is closer to non-Hindu China than the "Hindu India". India's Brahminical rulers are experts in making enemies because they are driven by the hate-filled Hindu heart.

You must make a study of these serious contradictions in the behaviour of the "Hindu Mind".

Privatisation

They say "we must love the motherland". But all those who run away to US, England and other European countries for "higher studies" and later settle down there are these upper castes only. Hardly 100 years ago a Brahmin leaving the shores of India was ex-communicated. But today, it is just the reverse. Every Brahmin family has one or two members in the US. Many marriages take place in foreign lands only. Displaying foreign car, foreign camera, handkerchief, foreign underwear, drinking Scotch whisky has become a status symbol. A "foreign wife" is a great asset. A non-resident Indian (NRI) gets better treatment inside India than an Indian living in India. What happened to their "nationalism"? All bogus. Pilots, scientists are threatening to take up jobs in foreign countries. What happened to their patriotism? All bullshit. Talk *swadeshi* and drink *videshi*.

When Brahmin Prime Ministers like Nehru and Indira Gandhi ruled India, the very same Brahminical people were in the forefront of state takeover of industries and banks. But within 20 years, the same Brahminical heroes went on a reverse gear — privatising anything and everything. By nationalising industries and banks then, they were able to take hold of top positions in all these establishments and later by privatising they could further entrench themselves. Both nationalisation then and privatisation today served the Brahminical interests.

Gandhi, the Father of their "nation", advocated *swadeshi* and driving out the British and all aliens. But the children of Gandhi are today busy inviting every Tom, Dick and Harry in the West to India and offering him the best facility to run the country.

Such serious contradictions can be found only among the "sick" rulers of India.

The problem is their sick mind is corrupting the whole country. It is high time that we the principal owners of India get this mentally sick people admitted to mental hospital.

Two sets of law

India is the only country in the world where we have two sets of law: one for the rulers and the other for the ruled. If a poor man out of hunger, unemployment steals a fowl, he is caught, handcuffed, called a "thief" and lobbed in the jail. His picture is published in the press and the name mentioned.

But if a "rich" man does not pay billions of rupees tax, he is given *Padma Vibhushan*, all sorts of awards and rewards. Upendra Baxi, a jurist (*Statesman*, Feb.18,1989) told a Delhi meeting that out of the 200-odd judicial commissions of inquiry relating to corruption charges in high places not a single one had so far resulted in conviction.

Karunanidhi was convicted by a judicial commission but became the Chief Minister again. R.K. Hegde was convicted by the Karnataka High Court and the conviction was upheld by the Supreme Court —apart from the dozens of other charges. But the Janata Dal, which once kicked him out, re-elected him to lead Karnataka. No political leader or religious leader was so far convicted and sent to jail. The examples are Satya Sai Baba, Jayendra Saraswati, Chandra Swamy and lots and lots of lesser fellows.

No film star has been so far sent to jail for not paying tax. They talk of socialism but their heart is in USA. They send their children to USA for studies. Our leaders go to US hospital for treatment. Even our marxist leaders like EMS Namboodiripad, Jyoti Basu take treatment in foreign hospitals. They say they are "nationalists" but want to possess articles and goods made in USA and Japan. Only a "Hindu mind" can have such serious contradictions.

Dual education system

We have two types of education. Expensive "private" convents and schools with English-medium education for the ruling class. Such schools and colleges get no government grants and hence no reservations for SC/ST students. Being expensive, no poor student can get admission. Public schools are exclusive to the "rich". The rest go to municipal or govt. schools and colleges where the medium is the mother-tongue. But in public schools the medium is English. Expensive schools where the rich and the mighty study (are owned privately) but called "public schools". But the schools where the poor children study in government-run schools are called "private schools".

Two types of drinks

We also have two types of drinks (liquors). The "rich" drink Scotch or what is officially named "Indian-made foreign liquor", manufactured by private sector distilleries. The "poor" are given the adulterated government toddy and arrack so that they will quickly get intoxicated and die early.

They say *Matru Devo Bhava* (meaning the mother is god) but treat the woman as slave. Then we have the "rule of law" and the "rule of the Manu". The woman is regularly burnt. *Sati, Devadasi,* child marriage, dowry deaths, caste system, *puja* in every govt. office, TV *Ramayana, Mahabharata* are all promoted because of the law of Manu. Shankaracharya of Puri defended Untouchability and *Sati* as per the Law of Manu. Indira Gandhi as PM was not allowed to enter Puri Jagannath Temple because of this laws of the Manu.

The Constitution of India "upholds" democracy, socialism and secularism. It is built on the foundations of justice, liberty, equality and fraternity.

But the laws of Manu are opposed to the rule of law but the ruling class wants to maintain the "Laws of Manu" for the benefit of our 15% Hindu rulers.

Sex crazy people

Brahminical religious scriptures make much of morality, charity, celibacy, character, abstinence, renunciation of sex, *brahmacharya,* saintly living, dignity of woman and what not. But the Indian films will not run without a rape scene. Go to any Hindu temple sex spills on its walls through stone carvings and pictures.

Hindus are the most sex-starved people in the world. Their own temple carvings are a proof of their sex perversion. *Kama Sutra* is the highest sold book in airport book stores frequented by our upper caste elite.

The wonder of all wonders is that our temple carvings are advertised as "Indian culture". What a sexual perversion? Look at the contradiction of this ruling class. Kissing is said to be prohibited in Indian cinema but rape is encouraged. This is because humiliation of the woman is part of the upper caste ethos which every day swears by *Mathru Devo Bhava*. But not a day goes without one upper caste woman being burnt alive for dowry or some other reason. Brindavan (in Uttar Pradesh) is bursting with upper caste widows. Mohandas Karamchand Gandhi beautifully portrayed this contradiction in the Hindu mind, said Sudhir Kakar, a leading psychiatrist, who examined this aspect of Gandhi. "Well-known" for his *brahmacharya*, Gandhi used to sleep with young girls. When his father died, Gandhi admitted in his autobiography that he was engaged in sex act in the next room. Gandhi symbolises the kink in the Hindu mind. (*Gandhi You Do Not Know*, DSA-2008, pp.76).

Double-think on liquor-drinking

Liquor is a taboo in India. Gandhi brought "prohibition" and Morarji Desai, a Nagar Brahmin from Gujarat, stretched it too far. Drinking is strictly prohibited and those who drink are called bad people. In all state functions, no drink is served. A visiting head of state is proposed a toast on *nimbu pani* (lime juice). All the Hindu VIPs who come to this function drink at home and come for dinner. Anybody who drinks is called a drunkard and his future is ruined. A deputy chief minister of Maharashtra (Congress Party) once lost his post for having been found drinking. What a punishment? But this is all for public show. In private all upper castes love drinking. Over 85% of the Indian people drink and drink is their daily diet. Except Muslims, who have a religious prohibition, all others drink and the drink is part of their life. But the ruling upper castes make prohibition an obsession. In all govt. parties, liquor is not served. Any driver smelling liquor is caught and fined. Jawaharlal Nehru and Sardar Patel, the two chief lieutenants of Gandhi, were liquor addicts and they had their daily peg even while staying in Gandhi *Ashram* at Sabarmati. All this perfectly fits with the upper castes. They never found fault with Gandhi, who did not drink, nor with Nehru who never missed his Scotch.

Meat, fish, chicken, pork, beaf are all food. It is the food of the millions and millions of SC/ST/BCs and Muslim/Christian/ Sikhs. But this food of the over 95% of the Indian population has no name. If at all it has a name it is a negative name. Their food is called "non-vegetarian". But the food of the Brahmin and a couple of others — not even 3% of India — has a name: "vegetarian". The food of the 95% of India is "non-vegetarian". It has no name.

Only a Hindu mind is capable of this gimmick.

Indians are meat-eaters

This "negative" name is given to frighten us and impose their vegetarian values. Rather, such a name is given to express contempt for our food so that we hide what we eat and feel ashamed. Many Dalit meat-eaters publicly announce they are "pure vegetarians". The Brahmin game is to make us hate our food, our names, our deities, our culture, our ancestors. When you hate yourself, there is no need for outsiders to kick you. You jump into hell yourself. The job is done.

SC/ST/BCs and Muslim/Christian/Sikhs are all strict meat-eaters. Over 95% of the Indian population is "non-vegetarian". All over the world people eat meat. These Hindus are trying to impose their "culture" on the non-Aryan Indians. This anti-meat-eating campaign is part of the Aryan cultural aggression against us. (*Aggression on Indian Culture*, DSA-2001, Rs. 50).

American cow

But you must know that during the Vedic period, the right of eating beef was reserved only for the Brahmin. All *vaidiks* now settled in USA eat cow. But if you point out this, their defence is: "We eat only the American cow which is not our mother". That means only the Indian cow is their mother. What logic? Only a "Hindu mind" is capable of manufacturing such a logic.

Even today in Kashmir and Bengal, Brahmins serve meat as *prasad* in temples. When Indira Gandhi as Prime Minister went to Dakshineswar, the "holiest temple" in Calcutta, she was served the meat *prasad*. What do they mean by vegetarianism?

There is a sinister design behind their "vegetarian" propaganda. Several days are declared by the government itself on which slaughter of animals are prohibited. Such a ban hits hard the Muslims who being butchers are deprived of their livelihood. The Brahminical vegetarianism is intended to hit the Muslim stomach. Even Dr. Babasaheb Ambedkar birth anniversary is declared a "no-meat" day by the government. The Hindu hate-filled heart must be taught a lesson. We can make them stop playing with our lives only if we make a careful study of the "Hindu mind".

Hindus must stop imposing their alien Aryan culture on us. It did not work in the past 4,000 years. Nor will it work today.

Aryans and non-Aryans

SC/ST/BCs and Muslim/Christian/Sikhs together forming over 85% of the Indian population will for ever and ever fight this Aryan cultural aggression. They may continue their enslavement technic. They may refine and make it more and more subtle and sophisticated. But they must note that the Aryan population in India was less than 15% over 4,000 years ago and even today they continue to be less than 15%.

This 15% includes the meat-eating stupid *shudras* who form over 10% of the Hindu population. The *shudra* Marathas, Jats, Patels, Vokkaligas, Reddis and Khammas, Nairs and Mudaliars etc. once fought only the Brahmins until they were co-opted after the "independence".

That leaves the three twice-born *dwijas* —Brahmin, Kshatriya and Vaishyas —who are a mere 5% micro-minority and hated even by their loyal *shudra* dog. Even among these three twice-born *varna*, the Kshatriyas are meat-eaters. Where then are the vegetarians in India? By enforcing vegetarianism, the Brahmins stand to gain nothing except the hatred of the entire country.

And we continue to be 85%. On the other hand, everywhere and on every front, the Brahmins are losing. Anything the Brahmins touch becomes mud.

Two separate nations

We two — the indigenous people and the alien Aryans — are separate and two different nations. They are *savarnas*. And we are *avarnas*. They are Hindu. And we are non-Hindu if not anti-Hindu. They are Aryan, we are non-Aryan. They are foreigners, we are the children of this soil — *Mool Bharatis*. We are *Bahujans* and they are *Alpajans*. The two can never meet, never mix and never compromise. The fight between the two began over 4,000 years ago. This fight continues even to this day. And it will continue for ever and ever until they stop their aggression on us.

If the Hindus are interested in peace, co-existence, unity and integrity of India, please cooperate or else you will be held responsible for inviting the charge that you are anti-national.

For heaven's sake stop this empty, meaningless, irrational controversies on non-issues like vegetarianism, abattoir, Narmada, Chipko. And let us together get down to build India.

But I don't think the Hindu sick mind will allow them to understand this.

Idli-sambar walas

Marwadis in league with Brahminical people engineering *Prani Daya* movement say vegetarian is the "healthiest food". But it is this vegetarians — *idli sambar walas* —who went to the different Olympic Games and ate dust there. It is our beef-eating Black Dalits who won all the gold. It is our Dalit girls — P.T. Usha, Shiny Abraham, Valsamma — who brought us all the medals. Why the vegetarianwalas did not get any gold for India?

Don't talk stupid things. In the international field of competition, such vegetarian values will take you nowhere. People will laugh at you. You may give a lecture on vegetarianism and draw big cheers in a "Rotary Club", "Lions Club" or "Donkeys Club" or a "Monkeys Club" inside India but when you go out of India you are judged by your efficiency, merit and strength.

China & India

Our vegetarian heroes speak about China and how China is "kind" to animals. They are bluffing. I had been to China twice. In China, all birds, wild animals, insects and dogs, cats etc. are shot dead. I did not find even flies, mosquitoes or bed bugs. This is because China says it is a "poor country" and they cannot afford to feed the animals, with their over 1,000 million human population. In the Brahminical "non-violent India", our pot-bellied "rich" upper castes feed pigeons, rodents, rats, monkeys, serpents, ants etc. to gain *punya* but starve the human beings. This is the difference between China and India.

"Animal lovers" often criticise the "reckless killing" of animals in India. But they do not speak about the reckless killing of human beings — at Moradabad, Meerut, Jamshedpur, Belchi, Parasbhiga, Nellie, Gujarat Genocide-2002. Muslims and Dalits are killed daily. Why can't the "animal lovers" have for a change some sympathy for human beings? We can understand all these tricks. It will not work. You must stop this nonsense.

Farmers who rear animals also love their animals. Those who breed animals have also the right to slaughter and eat them. "Animal lovers" don't breed animals.

These Goenkas, Birlas and Dalmias speak only about *Prani Daya* (kindness to animals) not because they love animals. They don't mean what they say. They don't say what they mean. The whole thing is aimed at fooling the SC/ST/BCs and instigating these innocents against the Muslim/Christian/Sikhs.

That is why I say: please study this mentally unsound "Hindu mind".

Please don't divide this country again. We SC/ST/BCs and Muslim/Christian/Sikhs —who form over 85% of the country will not give up meat-eating. If you want to be grass-eaters, we have no objection. But don't impose your vegetarian values on us.

But if you persist with the power of your "national" toilet papers, we will resist it with the power of our numbers. And in this fight if the country's unity and integrity — of which you are so much worried — suffers, the responsibility is on you. ■

----

2 – "Hindu unity" possible only when Brahminism is dead

As per the constitution of India, the Scheduled Castes (SC) and Scheduled Tribe (ST) are Hindu. The Hindu terrorist party, RSS, and its political wing, *Brahmana Jati Party* (BJP), also angrily assert that Dalits are Hindu:

Garve se kaho hum Hindu hai.

So, there is a total unanimity on the subject that we are Hindu. When we are Hindu, we automatically get every right to criticise our religion. The Hindu terrorist party also welcomes such internal criticisms on the ground that it strengthens the religion. Wonderful.

So the "criticism" made in this book should be treated as such though our Father, Dr. Babasaheb B.R. Ambedkar, said "the Untouchables (SC) are not Hindu and were never Hindu".

People greater than religion

As the Editor of *Dalit Voice* for 27 years and earlier 25 years in English daily papers, I had a long career of over half a century in Indian journalism, travelled all over India many times, met the country's most oppressed sections in different parts, lived with them, studied innumerable books — both Indian and foreign — and also written scores of books, had long discussions with thinkers and scholars. And at the end, my conclusion is if this huge country of over 1,000 million people must live honourably, Brahminism, parading itself in the new garb of Hinduism, must die. There is no other alternative. The people are greater than this so-called religion which is operating as a guillotine.

The book deals with the different mental diseases afflicting this ancient country which despite 61 years after "independence" is getting into deeper and still deeper crisis.

And yet its Brahminical rulers (15%) are not only not bothered but floating in their own dreamland giving all sorts of false hopes to the starving masses. Their favourite whipping boy is the country's 15% Muslims. All their false propaganda, their war and violence against Muslims may temporarily help them to *hinduise* (enslave) the non-Hindu Dalits, Backward Castes and Tribals and instigate them against Muslim. But whenever the elections come all these SC/ST/BC castes vote for their own caste candidate — breaking the "Hindu unity". In other words, the Brahminical rulers are not winning their war against India's Muslims. Muslim population is steadily and silently going up. The Hindu terrorists do not know that their hate-mongering is actually expediting the Islamisation of India.

Sweet talk of corruption

As the (15%) Brahminical upper castes have captured all levers of power — political, economic, social, education, cultural, religious, media, judiciary, scientific, military and security apparatus — they have suppressed any statement of truth coming out. Free breathing is not permitted. Anybody daring to question them is mercilessly crushed. So much so justice and truth have no place in this country. Every section of the society is headed by the choicest super Brahminical leech, one excelling the other, whose only job is to see that Brahminism is promoted by crushing any non-Brahminical forces raising their heads. Non-Brahminical sycophants trying to worm up will be happily encouraged but only after milking them dry and finally shot down fully disgraced.

Corruption is the sweetest talk of the town and the Brahminical media covers "corruption stories" but the corruption they talk about is the "money corruption" which is the last and the least form of corruption. But none is allowed to talk about the most serious form of corruption, namely the intellectual corruption, which breeds all other forms of corruption. (*India's Intellectual Desert*, DSA-2000).

By this time (2008) the country with its vast human resources (1,200 million), vast physical size and abundant natural resources should have become a leading country in the world. Neighbouring China is well on its way to become a super power but India continues to be a beggar country. Our megalomaniac Brahminical rulers flying in the cloud of 9% - 10% growth rate (GDP) are simply unstoppable.

Moneyed people respected

The most important cause of our decay and demoralisation is our irrational "Hindu mind" steeped in superstition, controlled by the Brahminical masters. At every state we suffer from a mental block. The only mantra that has gripped every "Hindu mind" is the get-rich-quick mania. Whether it is the father, teacher, friend, any elder, media, the only advice that you get today is to make money. "Make money as quickly as possible by hook or crook and that will bring you everything: fame, name, happiness, status, power, respectability". So much so every youth today is desperately rushing to make that quick buck. And the Brahminical society assures him money if he is ready to forget all those time-honoured values of Justice and Truth etc. India'a trash media very often front-pages pictures of the country's richest. And all these filthy rich are promoted as our new role models, nay saints, whom we are called upon to emulate. Nobody asks how they have amassed so much of money.

Such a Brahminical model is described as the money-driven society which is driving the "Hindu India". That means all that Budha, Nanak, Phule, Narayana guru, Periyar E. V. Ramaswamy, Dr. B.R. Ambedkar etc. have said — value-driven society — are dead.

This book deals with such a disaster facing this unfortunate country where we find hardly any soul ready to hear our voice. There may be a worried solitary soul here and there but that person lacks the courage to speak out. Brahminism has throttled to death all free thinkers. India's academic world holds the best example of such a vast intellectual desert where mediocrity is encouraged and full flowering of genius is crushed. India did not get a single Nobel Prize after "independence". Those "Indians" who did get the Nobel do not live in India — but foreign nationals.

Budha, the greatest Indian

In my long career of over 50 years in this vast intellectual desert, I have seen the Brahminical people systematically suppressing, if not eliminating, any dissent, any protest against their hegemony. As they are the lords of the land with every power in their hands they can easily do it. With the media as their deadliest weapon they can shoot any dog and call it mad.

If we go through the long history of India's turbulent past the only silver lining we get is that of the Budhist period when Brahminism was totally suppressed. That is how Budha is unanimously hailed as the country's greatest liberator and Budhism became its national religion — though Budhism, strictly speaking, cannot be called a religion as it denies existence of god. Budhism not only united India for the first time but gave its most glorious period in history which drew profuse praise from many Chinese pilgrims. At a time when the whole of Western world was unheard of, Asoka produced the "greatest nation of the world".

And the credit for killing this world's "greatest civilisation" goes to Brahminism. Brahminism infiltrated Budhism, divided it and destroyed it within India and drove it out of the country.

This is the beginning of India's downfall which got further accelerated after the very same Brahminical people used M.K. Gandhi to launch their fake "freedom struggle" to "drive out the British" and then imposed their Brahminical rule over India. The very forces killed Gandhi as soon as he installed India's first Brahmin Prime Minister and then onwards it was a smooth non-stop drive to re-establish their Brahminical hegemony over India.

With a micro-minority of 15% upper castes led by its 3% Brahmins establishing their hegemony over the rest of the 85% population how any just rule is possible?

Muslim rule

The one and the only sane voice that warned the country against the resurgence of Brahminical imperialism if the British were to quit without adequate safeguards was that of Dr. Babasaheb B.R. Ambedkar. But the Brahminical forces impatient to grab India and re-impose their imperialism, got the country divided — so that Muslims and Dalits — their two blood enemies— do not unite and thereby frustrate their dream of drowning India in Brahminical hell.

Under the Muslims (800 to 1200 AD), who knew nothing of the Indian social structure, once again the Brahmins emerged as the undoubted aristocrats of the country, leaders of the people, owners of wealth and power — and at the same loyally serving the new Muslim rulers with the hidden daggers ready to kill.

The sudden disappearance of Budhism and the passing of power into the hands of alien Muslim was a great blessings in disguise to the cunning crooks. It was a magnificent triumph of Brahminism. As the Muslims were totally new to India as invaders, their only interest was to rule and amass wealth which the Brahmins fully ensured as rest of the human activities were left to their care.

"Hindu" name selected by Muslims

Today the same Brahminical people's sole single slogan is to kill the Muslim and destroy his property. But the very same Brahmins had then welcomed the Muslim invaders, became their loyal dogs and instigated the Muslim rulers to break the back of the native rulers. The Muslims, whose rule was fully facilitated by the Brahmins, in turn surrendered to Brahmins and helped bring the entire country under the supremacy of Brahmins. Until the arrival of Muslims, the Brahmins were merely priests of the three upper castes — Kshatriya, Vaishya and *Shudra*. The Muslims facilitated the extension of the Brahmin hold on the rest of the population — namely the non-Hindu Dalits, Backward Castes and Adivasis (Tribals). Not only that. The Muslims gave the non-Muslims of India a new name: "Hindu".

The credit for making the non-Hindu original inhabitants of India as Hindu goes to the Muslims. "Hindu" was a name which no "Hindu" used in India then, and a name which was never used in any of the "sacred scriptures" of Brahmins. In other words it was the Muslims who converted Brahminism into Hinduism and the credit goes to Muslims for giving the new magical word "Hindu" and "Hinduism". All those who were not followers of Islam overnight became Hindu and the country they lived became Hindustan.

It was during the Muslim rule the Brahmins manufactured new scriptures, forged old ones and concocted scriptures. Not even the *Rig Veda,* supposed to be the most ancient and the "most sacred", escaped the profane interpolators.

The Muslim rule brought the heyday of Brahminism. And the same Brahminism is today unleashing its hate against Muslims and Islam, killing Muslims in thousands, cursing them for anything and everything. Brahminism jumps from argument to argument. It has no consistency. It adopts arguments, theories, idioms — anything and everything — that suits its convenience from time to time. If tomorrow "Hindus" and "Hinduism" come in the way of Brahminism they will not hesitate to disown and discard it.

Hence this book is to make the gullible, unthinking followers of Brahminism to "Know the Hindu mind".

Kashi Brahmin insults Shivaji

It was during this period the Brahmins established their three powerful institutions of "temple", philosophy and the caste system with its ascending order of reverence and descending degree of contempt. The caste system since then has remained deathless mesmerising the unthinking SC/ST/BCs and making monkeys out of them.

Shivaji was a Marathi *shudra* of the Maratha caste but the credit goes to this one single ruler of the Central Indian empire to promote Brahminism. The way a notorious Brahmin from Kashi humiliated Shivaji, who in his craze to become a *Chatrapati* (emperor), allowed himself to be kicked on the head by a silly Kashi Brahmin, Gaga Bhata, so that he could concoct a genealogy that Shivaji was a Kshatriya descended from a Rajput family. Even such a powerful Maratha king was treated like a dust by an ordinary Brahmin.

Marathas steeped in Brahminism

A section of the Marathas today headed by Purushottam Khedekar of Pune is no doubt carrying on a powerful anti-Brahmin movement. He founded the *Shiva Dharma* movement to fight Brahminism. While we wish them all success and also associated ourselves with his movement, we want to impress the *Shiva Dharma* leaders that it is very difficult to destroy the Brahminical mindset of their own Maratha *jati* brothers and sisters who hate Dalits and Muslim much more than they hate the Brahmins. The Brahmin plays upon this contradiction in the minds of the Marathas and instigates the Dalits and BCs against them. The caste contradictions in the Indian society helps the Brahmins to keep us as their slaves. This is because we have made no attempt to study the "law of contradictions" without which we can't defeat the Brahmin and his Brahminism. As long as the Brahmin-hating Marathas are steeped in Brahminism, how can they fight the Brahmin? The Khairlanji massacre of Dalits in the Vidarbha region (2006) was a wonderful Brahminical experiment on caste contradiction that simply pitted the entire Marathas against Dalits in which the Brahmins stood by the Dalits and became heroes.

Sikh revolution

Sikhism was born to liberate the people of Punjab — through which Brahmins stepped into India — from Brahminism. It was a powerful religion which the last Guru Gobind Singh perfected and made it a military religion and struck terror in the hearts of Brahmins. No doubt Sikhism saved the oppressed people of Punjab. This became possible because of the beneficial influence of egalitarian Islam which was then reigning supreme in Punjab. Sikhism itself was almost 80% Islam. Sikhism liberated the entire Dalits and other oppressed castes and particularly the women. A Sikh with his majestic turban, flowing beard and a religious right to carry a long sword struck terror in the heart of the Brahmin, a born coward, and the feudal lords in the villages. Wherever there was oppression Sikhs appeared and solved the problem. That is how Sikhism simply swept Punjab and the surrounding areas — with the burning heart of the Brahmins waiting for an opportunity to strike and finish this military religion.

Is there any instance in history the Brahmins ever failed to finish their enemy? We have not heard or read any such thing. Even the mighty Islam is shivering in its shoes today in India. What about the tiny Sikhism confined to the North West?

Arya Samaj under a Brahmin, Dayanand Sarawati, did this job. Following the "independence" (1947) and Brahminism taking over the leadership of the country, the very first job they did was to finish Sikhism through the "Blue Star Operation" (1984) in which Prime Minister Indira Gandhi, a Kashmir Brahmin, killed thousands of Sikhs within the Sikh holiest shrine, Golden Temple at Amritsar and broke its backbone. Sikhism today is practically dead. The Sikhs themselves are killing each other. The Brahmins have beautifully managed the brother killing the brother and the rest of India enjoying the scene.

British rule

The British rule further strengthened Brahminism. The great French Christian monk, Abe Dubois says all this in his book, *Hindu Manners, Customs & Ceremonies* (Rupa & Co, New Delhi - 110002). Brahmins, who are good servants but bad masters, became the obedient slaves of the British, supplied them everything including their women and made the British rulers great patrons of Brahminism. Sir William Jones, a British judge in India, translated the *Manu Smriti* into English all in the name of encouraging the oriental philosophy which in fact had nothing to do with Asia or its indigenous people.

The Hindu law (meaning the criminal Brahminical law) was applied to the entire non-Hindu population and barring Christian, Anglo-Indian, Parsi, Sikh, Muslim everybody else became Hindu — thanks to the British rule. But the very same Brahminical people, who gained so much under the British rule, later impressed the victims of their rule that they waged a "freedom struggle" against the British. How do you like this? Not only the SC/ST/BCs became total slaves but converted them into slaves enjoying their slavery. All over the world there are slaves but these slaves are fighting their slavery. But here in "Hindu India" we have a unique set of slaves who are actually enjoying their slavery. The mind control over the slaves is so tight and total that they carry the slippers of the slave-owner with utmost devotion.

The caste system was perfected during the British rule. Untouchables were kept outside the compound wall of the temple but the Backward Castes were allowed inside the compound wall but outside its inner demarcation. The British rule offered a new life to "Brahminism raising the Brahmin to highest posts of power, profit and confidence". (Swami Dharma Thirtha, *History of Hindu Imperialism*, Dalit Book Trust, 2003, p.168).

However, we have to admit that it is the British rule that gave birth to Mahatma Phule, Dr. Babasaheb Ambedkar, Periyar E.V. Ramaswamy, Sri Narayana guru — all revolutionaries. More than anything else the British rule offered the liberating Christian brotherhood. The British introduced for the first time science, education, industry, scientific administration, sociology, post and telegraph, the revenue system and many more. Though this country benefited a great deal from the modernising methods of the British rule, the best beneficiaries of the British rule were the Brahmins.

Three pillars of Brahminism

In other words it is the British who gave a legal sanction to the world's worst form of Brahminic satanic caste-rule under which the Dalits became the worst sufferers — Untouchable, unseeable, and even unthinkable.

The British helped the Brahminical people to establish the three most dangerous institutions in which the Bahujans today are caught and ground to dust daily — (1) caste system, (2) temple, (3) mutt.

Brahminism is promoting itself through these three institutions which with the awful funds at their disposal today serves as the inseparable fortress protecting the Hindu terrorist Rashtriya Swayamsevak Sangh (RSS) which set up the Vishwa Hindu Parishad (VHP) to guard the three pillars of Brahminism.

And in this task of promoting Brahminism, which is enslaving the 65% of the country's SC/ST/BCs, the one people who are unconsciously serving the cause are the Muslims who form 15 to 20% of our population.

Brahminism is managing the Hindu-Muslim divide and thereby protecting and promoting its cause periodically instigating "Hindu-Muslim" bloodbath. As I have written enough on this subject, I don't want to elaborate. But one thing has to be said that under the "Hindu rule" established over India following "independence" (1947), the Hindu-Muslim conflict is actively promoted by the state itself. In any other country the state can solve any conflict. The state has the force to intervene and stop any human conflict, war and violence. But in "Hindu India", the state itself actively aids and abets such a conflict. The most famous two examples: "Blue Star Operation" (1984) by the Brahmin Prime Minister Indira Gandhi and Babri Masjid demolition (1992) with the active connivance of the country's very Brahmin Prime Minister, P.V. Narasimha Rao. Hundreds of such cases are there on record.

Conversion to Islam

The pity is the Muslim leadership is not realising (or not interested in) the fact that they are helping the Brahminical rulers who run the state. The Muslim leadership even today calls the non-Hindu SC/ST/BCs as Hindu. They even call India as *Hindustan*, a name rejected in the Constitution of the country itself. What a misfortunate that the Muslim leadership, born and brought up in India for centuries — and converted from these very SC/ST/BCs — have not yet understood India and its social structure and its history. It is this appalling Muslim ignorance of India that is made use of by the Brahminical rulers to periodically stir up

"Hindu-Muslim blood bath" which help them to consolidate their imperialism.

Had the Muslim leadership of India understood the history of India, invited the oppressed Bahujans to their doorless masjid and into their glorious *Quran*, there would have been a stampede to get into the masjid. Already the Muslim population of India is 15 to 20%. Everyday more and more oppressed are getting converted to Islam. But once the Muslim leadership like the Jamate-Islami, Tablighi Jamat, Jamate-tul Ulama etc. declared the Dalits are not Hindu and were never Hindu but their brothers and it is the mere micro-minority upper castes (15%) who are persecuting the Dalits there will be a stampede into the masjid. But alas the leadership of all the Indian Muslim organisations is also under the mental control of the Brahminical people. The zionists who control the Arab oil-rich countries are exercising their influence through the leadership of Indian Muslim religious organisations.

Dalits don't hate Muslims

When I went to Pakistan in 2007 the Muslim leadership there was shocked to hear that the Hindu population of India is a micro-minority of less than 15%. And the rest of the 85% are also victims of Brahminism like the Muslims. But the Indian Muslim leadership is not interested in knowing this truth. Because the moment they tell the Truth, Truth itself will liberate the Muslim masses from the clutches of this handful of elite Muslim leadership.

To this day I have not heard any Dalit organisation complaining against Muslims. Dalits never hate Muslims. In every Dalit meeting all the abuses and criticisms are directed only at the

Brahmins. How can we say the Muslim leadership is ignorant? All the Muslim religious leaders of India read *Dalit Voice* and are familiar with our argument. Yet the Muslims think that we are Hindu. The ordinary poor Muslim is very friendly with Dalits. But it is the micro-minority rich, elite Muslims who are the culprits.

As the Muslim is fully under the control of their *ulema* (religious leadership) its ignorance of the "Hindu social system" is fully exploited by the Brahminical rulers. The day the Muslim leadership realises that India is not Hindu but actually anti-Hindu the burning anger of the Dalits will set fire to the Brahminical imperialism.

If India is suffering, choked to death by the Brahminical imperialism, part of the blame goes to the Muslim leadership — not the masses of Muslims who are innocent, good and superb revolutionaries.

Another partition of India?

India is sick. The caste system is killing us. Thinking itself has stopped. Ignorance and superstition, heaven, hell, *karma, punya* — all sorts of nonsense are having their dance of death and corroding and contaminating the life of every "Hindu". How then can the "Hindu" progress? The worst victim of the Hindu religion is the Hindu women.

Finally, one important point. The RSS-BJP Hindu terrorists repeatedly talk of "Hindu unity". But if there is one set of people who are working against the "Hindu unity" it is the Brahminical *vaidik* vampire. The caste system is not allowing the Hindus to unite. The one and the only section that is blocking the destruction of the caste system is the Brahmin. Dr. Ambedkar has made this point clear in his book, *Annihilation of Caste,* which was a speech he had to deliver at Lahore but was not allowed by the Brahminical hosts.

So who is coming against "Hindu unity"? Is it the Muslim? Christian? The Dalits? Nobody is against "Hindu unity". The one and the only person is the Brahmin. And without "Hindu unity" there can be no "Hindu-Muslim unity" or "Indian unity". Brahminical people are destroying every effort at "Hindu unity" because such a unity will throw the *vaidiks* out of the Hindu leadership. We will not be surprised that having lost Pakistan in the West and Bangladesh in the East, India will be subjected to further vivisection if this Brahminical terrorism is allowed to continue. Kashmir is boiling. The Mangaloid tribals of North-East do not consider themselves Indians. Violence is in the air. Any amount of military force, paramilitary, police etc. cannot "maintain the law and order" which the rulers want.

The way in which the Brahminical upper castes are going out of the way to welcome the American imperialists led by the zionists, we have the fear of the zionist takeover India with the active connivance of the Brahminism. But will China which is coming up at a breakneck speed allow this? Will not the nextdoor Muslim Pakistan join China to prevent such a take over and convert India into a major battlefield in the ongoing "clash of civilisations"? Are not the Brahmins in their mad, mad love to perpetuate their rule undermining the hard-won but fake "independence" of India? All these fears are giving us nightmares. ■

----

3 – Who is enemy of the Hindu?

The Hindu rulers are furious with the slaves of India that they are not being allowed to fly in the 8 to 10% GDP clouds. They say we are coming in their way. I have heard this complaint at many meetings and read it in news reports.

Their anger found expression in a *Times of India* page 1 editorial on the very opening day of the new year Jan.1, 2007. This was reproduced in full and I wrote an Editorial itself in the *Dalit Voice* of Feb.1, 2007: *"BSO divides India into two"*.

But those upper castes who are angry with us do not know that if India is nailed down and not allowed to fly in the GDP clouds, it is not because of us but because of the "hard work" of the very ruling Brahmin clique that is promoting religiosity, superstitions, blind beliefs through their flourishing god business, temple industries and the millions of godmen who are busy converting Indians into intoxicated monkeys.

Sick Western-educated Hindu

A *Hindustan Times*, CNN-IBN survey, conducted by the Centre for Study of Developing Societies (CSDS) comes out with shocking details that urban educated Indians are more religious than their rural and illiterate counterparts. Metropolitan educated women are more religious than rural women. Upper caste Hindus, fully exposed to modern life, are more religious than others. *Jalsa, Satsang, Rajyoga* are all very popular among the highly educated, Westernised Hindu. TV and English papers encourage these god business.

How can a country devoid of rational thinking, scientific values, logical analysis fly and float in 8% to 10% GDP clouds? How can hate-mongering promote fellow-feeling and team work?

Role models

Our scientists, educators, bureaucrats, IT wizards, film stars, cricketers — who are projected as our role model — are steeped in superstition and blind belief. Our politicians are still worse. Our godmen—we have millions of them— are a pest, a menace. Shielding the corrupt.

How can a country, wedded to such dangerous values make any advance on science and technology?

Progress of any country is possible only through science and technology which are enemies of superstition, blind beliefs. There is no other path to progress other than through science and technology. Our upper castes are the main beneficiaries of science and technology but they are also its worst enemies. It is they who throng to Satya Sai Baba, Ravi Shankar, Hare Krishna temples.

China's march

China today has surpassed India and joined the developed world because it is wedded to science and technology. But in India our rulers are not ready to give up even a single stupid superstition. Their Hindu religion is nothing but a stinking pond of superstition full of worms. Their religion is nothing but a bundle of dos and don'ts. Their gods and goddesses have all the human weaknesses. Show us one god who can be our role model.

Read Hindu terrorist party leader Arun Shourie's book, *Hinduism Essence and Consequence* (Vikas, New Delhi, 1979).

Hindu religion itself teaches no human values. The Hindu godmen have amassed Himalaya-high wealth with all their criminal records.

Kumbh mela

Not one Hindu "intellectual" has the courage to denounce all that is going in the name of their religion. Even the red hot communists of Kerala and Bengal are its ardent devotees.

Is it possible to keep all these dangerous anti-human values produced by this religion and at the same time make India fly in the 8 to 10% GDP clouds?

This is our point.

All the leading dailies and periodicals of India have their regular column on what the "stars" foretell, astrology, palmistry and all such rubbish. We have not seen one Hindu scientist denouncing the *kumbh mela* polluting the Ganga.

Every attempt is being made by our "highly educated" Hindu to keep the society in perpetual darkness, buried deep in the stupidest superstitions.

Science and technology have made hardly any strides in India only because of this strenuous Hindu attempt to kill the little remaining science.

Indian Institute of Science

The "prestigious" Indian Institute of Science in Bangalore, supposed to be the country's No.1 institution of international standard, is a den of *vaastu* experts, Sai Baba fans. Being a thoroughbred Brahmin institution it has never tried to root out all such activities that kill the little remaining scientific spirit in India.

At the same time all the staff and students of IISc are great admirers of "India shining" — renamed "India poised" by the *Times of India* — a Bania paper — getting ready to fly in the 8 to

10% GDP clouds. Our question is how can a country fly when it is nailed down to an antiquated and dangerous pig philosophy?

If progress is possible only through science and technology (every advanced society took only the same route) then we should be ready to get rid of every thought and action that comes in the way of such a progress. In the case of India it is Brahminism, which today hides under Hinduism, that is coming in the way of our progress.

Not the SC/ST/BCs or the Muslim/Christian/Sikhs who have better values.

God should be a model

This is our question to the upper castes (Hindu):

Do they subscribe to the Article 51A (H) of the constitution of India:

> "to promote scientific temper, humanism and the spirit of inquiry and reform"?

Has any scientific institute of importance like IISc discussed this Article and found fault with the godmen and Hindu temples violating the constitution and asked the government to punish such violators?

Hindus are not the only people in the world who have a god or gods. All religions have their own gods. Christians, Muslims, Sikhs, Parsis, Jews — all believe in god. And according to all these religions their respective god symbolises the highest virtues and values. Such a god combines in himself (or herself) highest qualities and possesses an unblemished, spotless character which are universally held as ideal and fit to be emulated by their followers.

The Budha, Jesus Christ, Prophet Mohammed may not be gods but prophets. So also Guru Nanak. But they all had a sterling character, led a noble life and fought for justice, truth and entire humanity. Every human being is proud of these prophets who have attained godhood because of their noble life.

A god has to be such a noble, super-human soul that parents could naturally ask their children to blindly follow the model of their god. While in distress, we say "Oh god" and we seek refuge in him. He should be such a noble person.

No god in any of the world religions is a womaniser —much less a fornicator. No god has stolen somebody else's wife. No god is a murderer. They were all personification of the purest and the noblest ideals.

Question to women libbers

How far Ram and Krishna, described as two of the greatest gods of Hindus, conform to this model of an ideal god? Dr. Babasaheb Ambedkar, the greatest thinker and scholar of "independent" India, naturally wrote his book, *Riddles in Hinduism* (*W&S*, Vol.4, 1987, Education Dept., Govt. of Maharashtra), to examine this very question: "Will Ram and Krishna as gods help the Hindu youth to become model citizens of India?" It is such a noble desire on our part to make India a powerful country and protect its unity and integrity that motivated us to reprint this book (*Riddles of Rama & Krishna*, DSA-1995), worried over the war and violence sweeping over the country following the Babri Masjid blast by the Hindu terrorists..

Will a mother tolerate her young son if he starts chasing every girl in town and then defends himself saying that he is after all following his favourite god Krishna? Will our women's liberation movement people excuse a man if he throws out his pregnant wife and defends his action on the ground that (like god Ram) he heard rumours about his wife's character and says there is nothing wrong in his action because his favourite god Rama did the same to Sita?

Our feminist leaders may excuse themselves saying that Ram's ill-treatment of his wife cannot be taken seriously because the *Ramayana* is not history and it is just a cock and bull story. Yes. If it is just a story, how did the Hindu terrorists demolish (1992) Babri Masjid claiming it to be Ram's birth place and that not a single Shankaracharya denounced this anti-national crime? Why the court itself entertained a petition on the Babri Masjid demolition which is still pending? Why did our fashionable feminists and their time-passwala women's organisations keep silent? Will our human rights people approve of Ram's killing of an unarmed, innocent Wali hiding behind a tree? If Ram is god why should he hide and kill Wali? How can a god believe in rumours on Sita when a god is omniscient and omnipotent?

Killing of shudra

Ram killing the Shudra Shambuka for no fault of the latter was such a horrible, such an unpardonable crime that it was cut even from the TV Ramayan that regaled the Hindu audience for months and months. The government feared that the young "modern Hindu" audience might revolt against this action of God Ram who killed an innocent Shambuka just because he performed certain Brahminical rites which as a *shudra* he was not expected to do. Can the killing of Shambuka be justified? Will those *shudras*, who are part of the Brahminical Social Order and form over 80%

of the BSO, excuse their own Hinduism for discriminating against Hindus? We thought the *shudras* (Hindus) might revolt against this act of Ram when they start understanding the meaning of this act of Ram and the Hindu terrorists defending it. But nothing of it happened because the Brahminical people have killed the very thinking power of all Hindus.

Hundred and one explanations can be given by defenders of Ram but no person with value for human rights can approve of it and *shudras,* who are also part of the Brahminical Social Order, will certainly revolt against Hinduism if the episode is properly explained to them. Babasaheb had warned the Hindus to take note of this serious offence of Ram.

Gandhi's *Ram Rajya*

And what a tragedy that M.K. Gandhi dreamt of establishing a *Ram Rajya* where shudras are slaughtered. Not only the "Father of the nation" fully approved of Rama's crime but described Ram's rule as the ideal and recommended India should be transformed into *Ram Rajya*. India indeed has become such a *Ram Rajya* where the Shambuks are slaughtered daily, with the full blessings of the "Father of the Nation". Right from day one of India's "independence" (1947), we have been on a slippery slope and finally we have come to the present state.

Deadly weapons

Did gods in other religions also commit such "human errors"? If Ram and Krishna were humans and not super-humans, how can human beings with all their faults and frailties be called gods?

A god is said to be embodiment of peace, compassion, love, justice, kindness. He doesn't favour one section of his people and discriminate against or kill another section of his believers. Why then Ram and Krishna (in fact all Hindu gods and goddesses) should carry deadly weapons in their hands?

Hindu religion, it is widely advertised, is the only religion in the world which stands for non-violence (*ahimsa*). If so, why the Hindu gods are carrying weapons? And against whom? Does the Christian, Muslim, Sikh, Budhist or Jewish gods carry such weapons? These questions are addressed to younger minds among the Hindus because the Constitution of India directs the state to make such an exercise under the above-quoted Article. Many young Hindus have not been properly explained about the facts of the case.

Perhaps the failure on the part of the state to implement the above-cited Article of the Constitution has led to the disastrous demolition of the Babri Masjid (1992) in the name of God Ram. It was a great human tragedy and a shame on India,. Thousands of Muslims (and Hindus too) were killed by the Hindu terrorists in the name of Ram. Earlier in 1984, the same Hindu terrorists demolished the Sikh's holiest shrine, Golden Temple, at Amritsar and killed thousands of innocent Sikhs. In 2002, the tragedy was repeated in the Gujarat Genocide.

Hinduism & nonviolence

Those who demolished the holy shrines of Sikhs and Muslims and killed thousands of Sikhs in 1984 and Muslims in 1992 said they were doing all this in the name of Hinduism. And the same Hindus say that theirs is the "only religion in the world that stands for "nonviolence and tolerance".

But the "Hindu mind" has stopped thinking and sees no inherent contradictions in the Hindu value system which has led the country from one disaster after another, turning it into a theater of perpetual war and violence.

Should not at least the coming generation of Hindus develop a scientific temper, questioning mind, rational thinking so that they could get charged with the task of pushing India into a modern, vibrant state? They must ponder over this question.

Do the Hindu youth of India feel there is nothing wrong with such a religion, gods, and their value system? Do they think the "Hindu mind" is sound? If so will their social system lead them to a healthy society? Will ridiculing and burning of Ravana, a Dravidian Budhist hero held in high esteem by a large section of the Indians, promote communal harmony? Is it proper to malign the robust Adivasis (10% of the Indian population) by giving a monkey face to their hero Hanuman? Is it proper to go on shouting *matrudevobhava* (mother is goddess) when Sita is suspected and forced to undergo fire-test every time? What will the 50% women of India feel about Ram's treatment to Sita?

Wanted a major surgery

Is it possible for "modern India" to compete with China and other rising nations without answering these questions? Should we not admit that there is something seriously wrong with our value system? Should not our religion and gods uphold truth and justice, humanity like all other religions and gods of the world?

Unless our value system undergoes a major surgery, India cannot rise —much less compete with others. And the value system of a society is shaped by its religion.

Young minds have to be trained to distinguish truth from untruth, justice from injustice, deeds from misdeeds. Scientific temper, rational thinking, logical arguments have to be cultivated right from the formative age. But how can such teachings impress young minds when our very religion and gods show a contrary path?

Worrying thoughts

Hindu religion is the cause of all our problems. Since the Dalits are also **called** Hindu under the Constitution, don't we have the right to criticise it? The appalling sufferings of the Untouchables, Adivasis, Backward Castes, Muslims, Sikhs and even upper caste women — over 90% of the population of India — do not send even a ripple in our hearts because our value system has made us heartless. We have become immune to all human tragedies. India has already won the notoriety of being called the world's most violent country.

How can we compete with China or any country with such a moth-eaten society packed with heartless and mindless people? Such thoughts are worrying us. ■

----

4 – Why Hindus could not produce an honest intellectual ?

Brahminical people may say that because we "hate" Hinduism, we are heaping all sorts of abuses only on Hinduism while being silent on Islam, Christianity or Sikhism. Such critics have not read our journal *Dalit Voice* or our books. How much we have criticised followers of these three religions also is all on record and we have any number of critics among these three religionists.

But this much has to be admitted that these three religions do not stand against science and technology as much as Hinduism. These religions do not have scriptural support to caste system or untouchability (racism). But Hinduism has any number of "sacred scriptures" which say that caste system and untouchability are the foundations on which this religion is built. That is why every Hindu temple enforces caste system and untouchability (apartheid) by preserving priesthood exclusively to the born Brahmins.

Caste identity

Dalits have their own complaints against these three egalitarian religions but we have no fundamental difference of opinion with them.

But Hinduism is north pole while the Dalits are south pole. We are the victims of Hinduism but not of these three egalitarian religions. Rather these three have liberated millions of our people in India. That is why we call them liberating religions.

Hinduism is oppressing us but the Untouchables at least are fighting back since centuries. The war is going on and it shall go on as long as Hinduism lasts. But what is worrying us is the plight of the Hindu victims imprisoned inside Hinduism itself. What we mean is Hinduism is killing Hindus themselves by not giving the Hindus any peace of mind. The Brahmins thought once they take over the over-lordship of India after driving out Muslims by partitioning India and killing Gandhi, they could establish their Brahminical *swarga* (heaven).

But this did not happen. Anything they touched since "independence" turned mud. Now with "caste identity" taking deep-roots the minuscule minority Brahmins have almost lost their political leadership. Brahmins must explain how their Hinduism helped the Hindu.

Why Gandhi was killed ?

M.K. Gandhi, the great *sanatani* Hindu, watered this Hindu tree and nurtured this tree so that nothing would grow under it. Gandhi and Gandhism are the other words for Hinduism. But the Brahmins shot dead this very person who did the greatest good to Hinduism.

It is under this Hinduism, Hindu temple, Hindu swamis (godmen), Hindu superstitions and all the above cited evils are flourishing. The moment you criticise it you are dubbed anti-Brahmin. Call the dog mad and shoot. This is the problem. Even M.K. Gandhi, who did so much for Hinduism was assassinated by a Brahmin only. Vivekananda who introduced Hinduism to the world was ridiculed and treated as an Untouchable within his own religious order, a Brahmin stronghold.

Why Vivekananda, Gandhi, Dr. Babasaheb Ambedkar and many others were hated? Because Hinduism is the other word for hate.

The hell that is holy Kashi

Look at our different religious centres — Brahmin, Muslim, Christian, Sikhs. We have visited the holy places of all these religions. We had visited Varanasi (Kashi), India's "holiest" place for Hindus on the bank of "holy" Ganga. You cannot find a more filthy place in the whole of India than Varanasi. If there is a hell on earth it must be Varanasi. How "India's holiest place" for Hindus became a hell? Who turned it into hell? Did Dalits do it? Or Muslims, Christian or Sikhs?

We visited the Puri Jagannath temple, which we had then described in *Dalit Voice* as "India's biggest mental hospital" (DV Edit April 16, 1997).

If you want to see racism in its most naked form you have to visit this temple. At its very entrance there is stone inscription warning that only a "born Hindu" is allowed entry. No Hindu court has found fault with this. Apartheid even in the 21st century. This most notorious institution which once belonged to the Orissa Adivasis was forcibly taken over by the Brahmins. Puri is not a Brahmin temple conforming to their tradition (*agama sastra*) is proved from the fact that the idol is made of wood, not stone. Prime Minister Indira Gandhi herself was once not allowed entry because the Kashmiri Brahmin married a Parsee. Dr. Babasaheb Ambedkar once took British Viceroy Mountbatten to prove the reigning racism in India. On March 4, 2007, the *Hindu* published the following shocking story of an American national detained by the police for entering the temple. Not only that.

Food buried in pit as American enters temple

Bhubaneswar: Food worth several lakhs meant as offering to deities at the Jagannath temple in Puri was buried on Friday

> morning following the entry there of an American national. Engineer Paul F. Roediger, who came to the holy town along with two Hindus, got into the temple without knowing about entry restrictions.
>
> The servitors raised a hue and cry over his entry, thereby disturbing the rituals. Roediger, who was detained by the police for nearly three hours, was allowed to go only after he paid a fine of Rs. 209. The food (*Bada Bhog*) was buried in a pit in a garden close to the temple. The temple premises were purified before the rituals resumed in the afternoon. As per the practice in the 12th century temple, only Hindus, Jains, Sikhs and Budhists of Indian origin or neighbouring countries are allowed entry.
>
> According to temple officials, this was the first incident in the history of the temple, where *Bada Bhog* was destroyed because of the entry of a person belonging to a different faith. According to sources, some foreign nationals were allowed entry way back in 1959 and 1960 but with permission from the Maharaja of Puri. Indira Gandhi was also denied entry as she had married a Parsi.

We had also visited Sikh's holiest shrine, Golden Temple, at Amritsar which remains spotlessly clean. We also visited any number of Muslim or Christian holy places —all well-kept, clean. But the filthiest, the ugliest and the most corrupt in the world are our Brahmin religious centres. Why? The Brahmins are so fastidious about cleanliness, purity, contamination. But their "holy" Ganga at Varanasi is flowing with burning dead bodies floating on wooden rafts. The water is stinking. The government gave the contract to a French firm which after years of efforts gave up saying that they failed. Why the "holy" Brahmins are not realising their own capacity to turn even nectar into poison?

V. Raghunathan, Managing Director of GMR, a Hyderabad-based company which runs the country's two biggest privatised airports at Bombay and Delhi, has written a book, *Games Indians Play*

(Penguin, 2006) in which he bitterly criticises the "elite Indians" for the state of affairs of this country. Who are these "elite Indians"? Who are the *Bhoodevatas*? Who constitute India's ruling class? Not Dalits, not Muslim, not Christian or Adivasis or even the OBCs. It is the upper castes — the top 15% of the Brahminical Hindus.

Are the souls of these "elites" revolting against these filth, the corruption, the disorder, the chaos at Kashi, Tirupati, Puri or at any Brahmin temple? Why? Because if they revolt against all these they will be hurting their own *jatwalas*? And there may be demands to "democratise" the *Devasthanams*. So they go on analysing, spelling out the symptom of the disease, hair-splitting, conveniently leaving out the diagnosis of the disease.

Hindu rate of growth

These "elites" are past-masters in blame game. If a bridge collapses or building falls killing many people they will quickly find a scapegoat but they will never own the responsibility. Their souls will never rebel at the disparaging reference to "Hindu fatalism". They will find hundred and one excuses but never pinpoint Brahminism as the sole single cause. Why? Because Brahminism is sacred and if that is touched the Brahmin will lose his leadership of the society, the country.

Raghunathan may be called one of the every rare intellectually honest persons we found among the upper castes to admit that the Indian "elite" has some major defects. He admits the spectacular progress of China in every field and particularly cities, the pan-Himalayan railway construction and calls it an engineering marvel. This stretch of 1,142 km was completed in a record four years and there was not even a single death. But the

18-km Calcutta metro took us 24 years. He calls it "Hindu rate" of doing things.

Then he talks of our "low trustworthiness", privately smart but publicly dumb, fatalistic outlook, being too intelligent for our own good, abysmal sense of public hygiene, lack of self-regulation and sense of fairness, reluctance to punish wrong doers, mistaking talk for action, deep-rooted corruption and a flair for free-riding, inability to follow or implement systems, a sense of self-worth that is managed only if we have the authority to break, finally the propensity to look for loopholes in laws. In all, he cites 12 "cannons" of Indianess.

Not identifying the "elite"

We don't say that these "cannons" are the monopoly of only upper castes. We can find plenty of Dalits, OBCs and even Muslim, Christian, Sikhs among the culprits. But who is the country's leader of thought and action? Who call themselves the *Bhoodevatas*? Who constitute the ruling class? Why the Brahminical Social Order (BSO) seeks precedence over every one else? Everybody follows the leader. If the leader himself is the culprit, if the fence itself eats the field who can save the society? This is the problem.

But even with V. Raghunathan there is a problem. He goes to the extent of booking the culprit and calls him or her the "elite". But the culprit remains nameless camouflaged as "elite" which is a meaningless effort. Raghunathan must be a deeply worried intellectual — otherwise he would not have taken the trouble of writing a book itself on the mess created by his own "elite" class. To that extent he can be called honest. But can he come under the definition of an "honest intellectual" (*India's Intellectual Desert,*

DSA-1999). Can he be become the scourge and scavenger of the society? We hesitate. Because he lacks the courage to **name** the culprit who is creating all the chaos and confusion in India. What is the use of summoning the doctor when the patient is critical and the doctor spends half hour examining the patient and then reads out all the symptoms of the disease, collects the fees but walks out without diagnosing the disease?

Will you be satisfied with such a doctor? V.Raghunathan is a fine doctor. He has honestly listed the symptoms — very detailed lists are given in his book. But he leaves us in utter confusion when he fails to diagnose the disease and name the culprit. This is the problem with him. He lacks the courage. Perhaps he fears that his own people may ostracise him. Perhaps he does not want to annoy his *jati* society, his people. It is this deep inner agony of the intellectuals, this dilemma not to confront their own people in the "elite" society that is perpetuating the "elites" and encouraging them to defy every law of the land and thus bringing bad name to the country itself.

Waking up the thugs

However, there is a plus point to his book. Because he did not name the culprit, even the culprit may read his book and enjoy the elaborate diagnosis of Raghunathan. Every thug and pindari would like to read and enjoy all about thuggery and highway robbery as long as he is not caught and punished. That is how all the thugs and pindaris themselves buy his books, read it, praise it, review it — and even give it awards and rewards. As long as the thugs and pindaris among the "elites" are not named and caught, there is nothing wrong in writing on thuggery and reading about it — all for entertainment.

Look at this amazing "Hindu mind". It gains name, fame and money by writing and speaking on thugs and pindaris and also by alerting and waking up thugs and pindaries. Both ways they stand to gain.

But the stinking society that is "Hindu India" continues well-entrenched as long as the culprit is not named, pulled out and mercilessly punished.

Why this "elite society" is not producing even a single honest intellectual who has the courage to be the "scourge and scavenger" of his own society?

This is the mystery of the "Hindu mind". ■

5 – Jews & the "Jews of India"

The Brahminical Order is a strange animal for which there is no parallel in the world. If there is one fantastic, mind-boggling bundle of contradictions in the whole world it is India's Brahminical *Bhoodevatas* (gods on earth).

During the British rule in India the *Bhoodevatas* felt terribly suffocated by the strict enforcement of the rule of law by the British. The Brahmin was treated like any other offender and sentenced. The British, however, empowered the Untouchables, and extended all-out encouragement to Dr. Babasaheb Ambedkar, an Untouchable. Having been accustomed to centuries of discriminatory practises and racism, the Brahmins were deeply upset by the British sense of justice and fairplay. So, they decided to oppose and finish the British rule having been convinced that the continuation of British in India would harm their interests.

Brahmin support to nazis

The Hindu terrorist party leader, M.S. Golwalkar's book, *We & Our Nationhood Defined* (Pharos Media, PO Box-9701, Abul Fazal Enclave, New Delhi -110 025, 2006, pp.160, Rs. 120) has all the proofs for the Brahmin hatred of the British. In this the Maharashtrian Brahmin openly supports Hitler and his nazi regime and even congratulates Hitler for killing the Jews.

Look at the intellectual dishonesty of M.S. Golwalkar. Even when he knew that the Chitpavan Brahmins were Jews why did he instigate German nazis against Jews? Does it not reveal the treacherous character of the "Jews of India"?

We have elaborately dealt with the Brahminical support to German nazis and Hitler, whom they hailed as an *avatar*. They gave the Brahminical symbol of *swastika*. We have devoted several chapters in our book, *Brahminism* (DSA-2002), to prove how the German nazi intellectuals were inspired by the Brahminical "sacred scriptures" and other Sanskrit literature which inspired many scholars like Nietzche and a galaxy of other oriental scholars who gave birth to the theory of Aryan race superiority. A top Jewish scholar, Leon Poliakov, has written a book itself (*The Aryan Myth*, New American Library, New York, 1977) pinpointing that Hitler and his nazi ideologues were inspired by India's Brahminical literature. (*Dalit Voice* April 16, 2007 p.20: *"Jews join very creators of Holocaust"*).

Germans taken for a ride

Brahmins had given all-out support to Hitler because they honestly thought he would come out victorious in the World War-II defeating the British whom they hated from the bottom of their heart for "ill-treating" the Brahmins. They even invited Hitelr to India and assured him a red-carpet welcome. Several German scholars visited India and many Brahmin scholars went to Germany. And the result was the establishment of a chain of Max Mueller Bhavans in all big cities of India. But in Germany itself nobody has heard of Max Mueller who became famous only in India because he translated all the "sacred scriptures" to English. Brahmins started studying German language and Germans started learning Sanskrit. This went on for several years. And the result was the innocent Germans were taken for a ride by the Brahminical cock and bull story. It is the Brahmins who injected the Aryan racial pride in Germans and the poison of anti-semitism which led to the so-called Holocaust and finally resulted in the creation of the zionist homeland of Israel committing aggression on the Palestinian territory and provoking the world's longest lasting (over 100 years old) Middle East Muslim mayhem.

We had pointed out all these and furnished all the proof of historical records of the Brahminical responsibility for engineering anti-Jew hatred by Germans in general and Hitler in particular who can be hardly accused of being anti-Jew. (DV Feb.1, 2007 p.21: "*Hitler was not anti-Jew: Zionists supported nazis*", Alan Hart, excerpts from the book, *Zionism — the Real Enemy of Jews*, 2005).

Leon Poliakov, the author of the monumental book, *Aryan Myth*, and a top Jewish scholar having criticised the Indian Brahmins and pinning the blame on them for poisoning innocent German minds against Jews, had refused to answer our star question: How the Jews, the victims of Brahminism then, are today all-out collaborating with their very oppressors?

We have cited hundreds of examples of the Jews and "Jews of India" coming together. The latest is the joint meeting of the Jews and the "Jews of India" in Delhi on Feb.17, 2007 (DV March 1, 2007 p.15: "*Brahminism & zionism join hands*") in the residence of L.K. Advani, a Hindu terrorist party leader.

Jews refusing to answer

The Jews claim they are the brainiest and the most brilliant in the world. They are also the ruling class of the Western world — controlling its finance, media, political machinery etc. Admittedly they are the most powerful people in the world today. It is these mere 3% of the American Jews who control the entire American administration and its entire life breath. If they are so brilliant and so far-sighted how did they forget the crimes of the Indian Brahminical people who instigated the Holocaust?

We had put this question many times and all the top brains among

Jews are well aware of our question but they are refusing to answer.

They are silent because their erstwhile oppressors have become their today's collaborators in jointly fighting the Muslims, their latest enemy.

The Brahminical people of India have neither a permanent enemy nor a permanent friend. They change according to the changing time. The zionist Jews do not know this. They do not know this because they have not made a study of the "Hindu mind".

Yesterday, the Brahmins used the German nazi's thinking that they could be used to fight and finish their enemy No.1 — the British. To fulfil their aim they manufactured an enemy to the nazis and Hitler and named the enemy as the Jew. Once their game failed and Hitler got defeated, they quickly shifted their side. Yesterday's enemy has suddenly become their bosom friends and the two bosom friends met in Delhi on Feb.17, 2007 to fight and finish their new enemy, the Muslim.

War against Islam

And the Jews think that the Brahmins, as the ruling class of the "rising Asian power", India, may be useful in tackling the Muslims against whom they are engaged in a life and death battle in the past 100 years or so.

The zionist-Muslim clashes started only after the zionists committed aggression on the Arab territory of Palestine to establish their homeland of Israel. And in their war against Muslims they managed to employ the White Western Christian rulers. It is the White Western Christian rulers who are fighting and killing the Muslims on behalf of the zionists. Except the brief period of Crusades, history has no proof of Christian-Muslim clash. But it is the zionists who misled the Christian ruling class to fight the Muslims.

White Western racists among the Christian ruling class at least are dutifully and faithfully carrying out the zionist order of killing the Muslims.

To that extent the Christian rulers have been faithful to their semetic religious colleagues. But the Brahminical people of India say they do not belong to the semitic religion. But our investigation reveals that the Jews and the Brahminical people originated from the same Middle East area and both are genetically same. That is how we called them the "Jews of India".

If the Brahmins are anti-semitic and hence anti-Jew, how their top secret book, *Arthasastra* (Dr. R. Shamasastry, Padam Printers, Mysore-24, 1988) and the zionist secret book, *Protocols of the Learned Elders of Zion* (Scientific Research House Kuwait, DSA-2001), have the identical objectives of tackling and eliminating their enemies?

When Jews were duped

How did such a galaxy of brilliant people fall flat before the cunning foxes who called themselves Aryans and bluffed saying they are anti-semetic and thereby finally causing the World War-II.

How the same Jews who caused the World War-II and preparing for a World War-III are believing the very people who once duped them and caused their slaughter (Holocaust)?

Alan Hart, a British historian and a specialist on Jews and zionism, accepted our theory and said this in his inaugural speech in

Bangalore (India) at a conference. (DV Edit March 16, 2007).

How can the Jews consider the Brahmins trustworthy today when their own zionist historian, Leon Poliakov, has directly named and accused the Brahmins as the sole single cause of Hitler's holocaust?

Be that as it may. We admire the Brahminists of India for having ditched and duped the world's brainiest people, namely the Jews.

After comparing the two, experts on the subject feel that the "Jews of India" are more dangerous than the Jews. The Jews at least have been consistent and put up a relentless fight for their cherished homeland.

Brahmins have no homeland

But the "Jews of India" had never fought for a homeland. Not one Brahminical intellectual had ever scientifically identified their homeland. Bal Gangadhar Tilak, the topmost Chitpavan Brahmin leader and a founder of the Hindu terrorist party RSS, had identified the Arctic region as their homeland. Somebody else called it the region somewhere around Iran. There was never a unanimity on this subject.

Nor did anybody in the world offered them a shelter to settle down. Ever since then these people — who originally called themselves Aryans, which is an umbrella name for the *varna* (colour), Brahmins, Kshatriyas and Vaishya — antagonised the original inhabitants of India and got involved in a perpetual, never-ending war with the India's Adi Dravidas and Dravidas. Of the three *varnas*, the Brahmins formed just 3% and even to this day after thousands of years, they continue to be 3% only.

The Jews at least settled themselves in several Muslim countries like Iran, Iraq, Syria, Jordan, Egypt and even to this day the Muslims had hardly any complaint against them. The Jews had their synagogues and all their religious activities. Muslims hardly had anything to complain.

But that is not the case with India's Aryan Brahmins in particular. Their first and the most ghastly crime was in destroying the Indus Valley Civilisation. And second was in destroying Budhism. ■

1. *Jews of India Getting closer to Jews* (Story of conspirators turning into collaborators), V.T. Rajshekar, DSA-2008.

2. *Brahminism in India & Zionism in West — Horror story of two world famous tyrants*, V.T. Rajshekar, DSA-2007.

----

6 - India becomes a sick nation

The Brahminical ruling class is India's opinion-maker, leader of thought and action, and the supreme lord of the land. People look to this class as their elder brothers to follow in their footsteps. If the SC/ST/BCs (65%) and Muslim/Christian/Sikhs (20%) — a total of 85% of the country's population —blindly follow any "leader" that leader is the Brahminical order. If the country has progressed and got the highest rating, the credit will go to this ruling class. If the country has collapsed and become a laughing stock of the world then also the credit has to go this class alone.

Values come from religion

But here comes a problem: the moment the shortcomings are pointed out, our Brahminical leaders are quick to hit back and say that all these problems are common to other countries also. Just because other countries also suffer from the same ills does not make India's disease any more acceptable. Their one favourite argument to rebut us is to cite "India's glorious past". But what is more important is not our past but our present. We might have produced the Indus Valley but that was the product not of the ruling Aryans but of India's indigenous people. Nor do what is referred to as the "golden age of Indian history" belong to the Aryans. That "age" belongs to the Budhist rule hated by the Aryans. Today's Brahminical rulers cannot claim credit for what is not theirs.

Rational thinking, logical analysis, scientific temper — where does it come from? All these flow out of our value system. If we are a set of people believing in astrology, palmistry, superstition, fatalism, *karma*, rebirth then we must know all these come from value system. From where does our values come? Values flow out of our religion.

Rationalists may not agree with this. They may say they distrust anything that contradicts science or outrages reason. They believe with certainty that an ethical life can be lived without religion. Karl Marx said:

> "Religion is the sigh of the oppressed creature, the heart of heartless world, just as it is the spirit of a spiritless situation. It is the opium of the people".

Hinduism, which is the current name for Brahminism, is the most irrational, unscientific and anti-human and also the most violent of all world religions. It is the Hindu value system that has caused so much of stinking garbage to accumulate in the Hindu brain. How can you ask Hindus to be rational keeping their value system in tact?

That is why no Hindu finds anything wrong in the Hindu god Rama killing Shambuka or the god Rama throwing his wife Sita into forest for 14 years. The Hindu never finds fault with Krishna stealing the dress of girls who got into a pond for bathing. The Hindus are told these are divine acts and made "to believe" it. Can a god commit a theft, a crime or any act for which a human being is punishable under the law of the land in India?

Govt. defends *karma kand*

That is how India has become a "sick nation". A Govt. of India Minister, Murli Manohar Joshi, a Brahmin, introduced astrology and *karma kand* in the university curriculum and there was no protest. He gave public lectures on their great scientific values and the country's Brahminical media faithfully reported it. None criticised him and the Minister lasted the full term. What happened to the "great scientists" of India?

He even gave a call as the Union Education Minister to introduce Hindi, Sanskrit and other Indian language for science teaching.

His argument is "Indian thoughts" taught in a foreign language could never be original. The talents would get frustrated if science is taught in English. During the Hindu terrorist party rule, Dr. Joshi was actively assisted by Vignana Bharati, a wing of the party, to bend the country's education system to propagate Brahminical values. No Hindu scientist opened his mouth even while attending such conferences.

The Hindu value system does not ask us to rebel. Hindu values ask us worship wealth. And all those Hindus who grabbed wealth did it by all types of illegal means. On one side we say means is more important than the ends but at the same time we worship the rich. Can selfishness lead to cooperation? That is how the cooperative society movement collapsed in India because our value system teaches not cooperation. It asks us to seek individual salvation. We are a selfish people.

Quick reply to defend any wrong

Only the Muslim, Christian and Sikhs have a collective prayer in their respective places of worship. But the Hindus have nothing like a collective prayer. Because they do not believe in collective salvation. They always seek individual salvation. Hindus are highly individualistic because of their value system. A Hindu goes to a temple either alone or with his wife and prays for his individual salvation — silently. But the other religionists go to their places of worship and collectively pray for the collective good of the whole society.

The Hindu finds nothing wrong in cheating or committing a fraud. Muslim, Christian, Sikh religions may also produce a similar cheat but rarely. For that the reply of the "argumentative Indian" is Hindus are large in population and so they produce large number of frauds. They have a quick reply to defend any wrong doing.

But look at the frauds of Harshad Mehta. He caused a total financial crisis and several banks collapsed. Was there any collective outcry? The *Times of India* offered him a contract to write a column. The Gujarati Bania was praised and paraded and called a financial wizard, "smart guy", a "shrewd businessman".

The then Finance Minister at the Government of India, Manmohan Singh, was fully aware of the entire frauds of the Gujarati Bania but he was praised and later promoted Prime Minister of India. Anybody supporting the manipulations of the "rich", who are invariably the upper caste (Hindu), is praised in India. But those working for the poor (means the lower castes) are dubbed terrorists, anti-socials — all sorts of names. Call the dog mad and shoot.

Corruption begins from top

There is no collective outrage, no collective protest. We simply put up with our unruly traffic, filthy streets, stinking toilets. Yes, we do complain without doing anything to correct it. Privately we grumble but publicly dumb. We want others to champion a cause. But we are silent. But who are these "others". We don't know that they are like us only, says Raghunathan and adds: "So we are left with a thousand issues facing the country and no champions in sight".

Our media is full of stories on corruption. Any corrupt person caught gets the widest publicity. The readers love to read corruption stories. What is the outcome: India is one of the most corrupt countries in the world.

Corruption begins from the top: the Prime Minister, Chief

Minister, Chief Justice, Director-General of Police, Army chief, Secretaries to government, vice-chancellors. But these top guys are not caught and that is how the corruption continues. The poor police constable, a junior hospital doctor, a sub-registrar is caught, paraded and the picture published on front-pages. And we think corruption is banished.

But what about the corruption in the Hindu temples? The list of temple corruption is announced in a huge board at the very entrance to the temple. If you give Rs. 20,000 "bribe", you can see the god straightaway. But if you can't pay, then you have to stand in the Q. Is this not corruption? Did we question it and punish the corrupt priests who are swallowing this money — without paying the income tax? What is the income of the temples? Did we demand income tax on their income? No, we will not do it because we can't interfere in "religious affairs". Because it is part of our faith and faith can't be questioned.

If your "faith" interferes with collective cause, can we remain silent? In the capital city of Delhi there are many temples which literally block the public roads and seriously affect flow of traffic. But no temple was demolished. And all the "Hindus" who also suffer are silent. And silently suffer. A temple, masjid or any place of worship cannot come in the way of public good. So much so our urban life has become chaotic. Too much noisy. During the *Diwali* even the Supreme Court judges, who are so much bothered about public discipline and order, are silent. When it comes to Hindu it is a collective conspiracy. And because of this collective conspiracy, the country has suffered. The holy Ganga becoming a stinking drainage flowing with gutter water can be cited as the best example of our collective conspiracy. ■

----

7 – The twist in "Hindu mind"

When a human being and our ancient ruler, Bali Chakravarti, attained great name and fame and all his subjects were adoring him, the Aryan "Hindu" gods became jealous and conspired to destroy him exploiting the Emperor's very goodness and generosity itself. Aryan god Vishnu was assigned this job of "finishing" the beloved Bali Chakravarti and he came disguised as a Brahmin "beggar". When the Emperor asked him to demand what he wanted, Vishnu, begged for just three feet land in Bali's kingdom. When the request was granted, he kept one foot on Bali's earthly dominion and the other foot on his "heavenly dominion". And then treacherously extending a third foot, he asked Bali as to where this third step be kept. Finding nothing left, the great generous Bali Chakravarti permitted Vishnu to keep it on his own head. And Vishnu kept his third foot on Bali's head and pushed him down into *patala* (hell). This is just a cock and bull story weaved by the Brahmin writers but the actual fact is it was a fight for land between the invading Aryans and the indigenous people, whose king was Bali.

Significance of Diwali festival

Bali, knowing that he has been treacherously overthrown and his end has come, asked Vishnu to take care of his subjects. Vishnu promised and told him that once in a year he could come back to earth and see for himself the joy and pleasures of his subjects. And it is to welcome Bali that *Diwali* is being celebrated all over India by lighting lamps, sparklers and distributing sweets. *Diwali* might have been now converted by the enemy to Brahminise our brains. But historical facts are that it is a festival to commemorate a great, benevolent indigenous king who ruled the whole of India.

This is not a laughing matter. "Hindu" mythology is full of such meaningless stories. Do not raise questions like from where Vishnu's third step came, whether the earth is shaped like a plate or a ball, why gods were so helpless etc. Do not also ask whether the pomp and pleasure shown during *Diwali,* on just one day in a year, will not amount to breach of promise as Bali's request was not confined to one day only.

Through this story we want you to get a peep into the "Hindu mind" and the helplessness of the Aryan (Hindu) gods and in particular show how the Hindu gods are jealous, cruel and deceitful.

Character of Christ

Compare the character of Aryan (Hindu) gods with the Christian "god", Christ (if he can be called god). He was nailed to a cross, full of agony and pain — bleeding. Why? He suffered to save his believers from the pain of hell. This symbol of Christ is a symbol of mercy and sacrifice thus conveying the message to Christians that Christ is mercy and mercy is godly and a good Christian should be merciful and is committed to fight and die for the oppressed and the persecuted.

Again, compare the Muslim concept of god. Every action is done in the name of Allah, the benevolent and merciful. This conveys the message that the greatness of a Muslim is in his being benevolent and merciful.

But the Aryan "god" is the symbol of jealousy, deceit and breach of promise, cruelty, tyranny, violence. Dr. Babasaheb Ambedkar has spoken about all these aspects in detail in his different books.

Sex-crazy gods

Not being content with this, various sex stories are attributed to Aryan gods. Indra, getting fed up with the *Apsaras* of heaven, desires to have sex with the most beautiful earthly women and deceitfully comes to Ahalya, the wife of Gautama in the guise of Gautama himself and indulges in sex act. It is again through the perverse sex adventures of both Vishnu and Shiva that Hanuman's mother Anjini becomes pregnant and delivers the monkey-faced Hanuman. Numerous such stories can be cited to elucidate this aspect.

Mind makes the man

Through this we intend to explain that those who read, appreciate and believe in such cock and bull stories start developing a particular mentality. Psychologists have much to say on this aspect and they cite many examples. The "Hindu" thought, action and approaches to issues are the living examples. It is the mind that makes the man. And the "Hindu mind" being what it is, we find the upper castes finding great pleasure in the pain of non-Hindus. Western writers being unaware of this "Hindu mind" have taken great pains to cite examples by conducting countless surveys and gathering information on the private affairs of individuals.

There is no need for Indians to make any fresh survey and gather facts. Plenty of facts and figures, every data are available and simply rotting in our store houses. Instead of wasting time on such surveys it is better we make a study of the "Hindu mind" which will give us a peep into what is India today. The characteristics of this "Hindu mind", temperament and action, daily seen around us, are sufficient to know and understand why

India today is facing such all-round confusion, crisis, violence and moral decay.

Rushdie's Satan

A prominent example of this pervert "Hindu mind" can be easily deciphered from the great rejoicing of the upper castes over Salman Rushdie's book, *Satanic Verses (Dalit Voice* Nov.16, 1988, p.7). A cheap writer, he took an advance of Rs. 2 crores from the publishers, the Jewish-owned Penguins, to write this trash and to satisfy the cheap sentiments and get praise from the upper castes. But he selected the wrong place, Mecca, though named as "Jahiliya", and allegorically took the names resembling certain personalities held in high esteem by the Muslims. For the heavy amount he took to write this gutter stuff, he had to cough up a higher price — the wrath of the entire Muslim world plus the curse of the entire saner part of the non-Muslims. V.P. Bhatia, editor of the Hindu terrorist mouthpiece, *Organiser,* suddenly developed sympathy for him and warned him to take care of his life. He cited the example of Ilamuddin who killed Rajpal, the author of *Rangeela Rasool,* in 1928. Why Bhatia (*Organiser,* Oct.23, 1988) recalled this incident and suddenly developed sympathy for Salman Rushdie? Anything that wounds the Muslim sentiment is dear to our upper caste "intellectual" prostitutes.

Then we have the equally famous example of the Bangladeshi sex writer Taslima Nasreen who has become the darling of the Govt. of India itself which treated her as a state guest. One single foreign woman has become more important than India's millions of Muslims who protested against her and demanded her expulsion.

Music to Hindu ears

Arun Shourie, once editor of the *Indian Express* (Oct.19, 1988), started writing all sorts of garbage stuff to bring about a rift between Muslims and Christians — India's two persecuted minorities. (DV Dec.1, 1988, p.12). Pains of Dalits, Muslims, Christians and Sikhs are music to "Hindu" ears.

Hindu religious leaders have not explained the most glaring contradiction between their claims of "non-violence", "tolerance", etc. and the violence and intolerance exhibited by their gods. Their gods and goddesses are debaucherous and their temples are dens of prostitution, surrounded by Devadasis and walls painted and sculptured with nude pictures.

But Muslims, Christians and Sikhs have kept their places of worship clean, pure and wide open to everybody. Anybody having a doubt can visit a mosque, church or *gurdwara* to check these facts. When that is the case, how could the Hindu terrorists attribute filthy things to Muslim, Christian and Sikh? They dare not do this. They are afraid of youths like Ilamuddin. But they wait for some one among the rank and file of these religious minorities to do this job. That is why they gloat over *Last Temptation* and the *Satanic Verses*. But both Muslims and Christians stand together against such sinister designs by internal saboteurs. Muslim organisations in UK and other Western countries have expressed sympathy with those Christians who opposed screening of the *Last Temptation*. This is because Christian opinion is divided on this issue. Muslims hold Christ in high respect and proudly name themselves as Isa Khan, Syed Isa, Shaikh Isa, Ghulam Isa, etc. Mariam (Mary) is a common name among Muslim women.

Nation equated with "Hindu"

During the Taslima Nasreen controversy gallons of tears were shed in India's "national" toilet papers over the "choking of freedom of expression". But these toilet papers did not write a single word when Babasaheb Ambedkar's *Riddles of Hinduism* (1988, Maharashtra Govt.) was banned and burnt and when the Quran was sought to be proscribed in the Calcutta High Court. Where was their concern for the "freedom of expression"? "What hurts others should be freely spoken and published but what hurts Brahminical people must be banned". This is their logic. Whenever they say that the "nation's unity and integrity is threatened" they mean the upper caste nation. This is what we call as the "Hindu mind".

Some Bhatias and Sethias have demanded a ban on our Dalit Sahitya Akademy books (DV Dec.1, 1988, pp.18). They suddenly forget that their own Hinduism has been the target of criticism right from the beginning of Hinduism. They always talk of "reforming" the Hindu religion. All "reformers" like Raja Ram Mohan Roy, Vivekananda, Gandhi, etc. are held in high esteem by these upper castes forgetting the fact that these "reformers" became famous only by criticising Hinduism. By reforming their laws, customs and manners these "reformers" have admitted that the Aryan-imported Hinduism is bad and still there are many bad things which requires to be reformed. Since "reformation" comes only after criticism and exposing the vices, such exposure and criticism must be welcomed and appreciated.

No. Brahminical people do not agree with this. They say these criticisms can come only from the twice-born *dwijas*. Others have no right to criticise Hinduism. Only that water that comes out of their *shanka* (conch) is *amrita*. Otherwise it is ordinary water. These upper castes fall head over heels to call us Hindu. According to them Scheduled Castes, Tribals and Backward Castes are also Hindu. Gandhi renamed them *Harijans*, children of god. But this is only to the extent of getting their votes and then rule them. These SC/ST/BC "Hindus" have no right to criticise their Aryan Hinduism. See the duplicity. This is what we call the "Hindu mind".

Hindus borrow Christian values

Hindus feel sad that they only talk of "reforming" their religion while Muslims and Christians never talk of reforming their religions. The reason they attribute for this is "Hindus" are very liberal, broad-minded, progressive, tolerant and accommodative while the Muslim, Christian, Sikhs are the opposite of it — "fundamentalists". However, they forget that while reforming their "Hindu" religion, what they borrow and adopt are Christian and Muslim values. It was Islam and Christianity that had influenced Raja Ram Mohan's reformation. Gandhi was influenced by Tolstoy. Democracy, socialism and secularism are borrowed from the West and implanted into the Constitution.

Such liberating values are not acceptable to the Hindu is different. But they are at least making a show of borrowing from non-Hindus which means their Hinduism is faulty.

They know their Hinduism is stinking but this right of saying that it is stinking is reserved only for them. This is "Hindu mind".

It is high time that Hindu terrorists stop gloating over frauds like Salman Rushdie and Taslima Nasreen and feel jealous of Muslims. Muslims know how to deal with their internal saboteurs.

The Rushdie and Taslima episodes should help the Muslim, Christian and Sikhs apart from SC/ST/BCs to make a deep study of this pervert "Hindu mind".

It is this twist in the "Hindu mind" that has caused all our miseries, and over 85% of India's population including Hindu women have become victims of this violent "Hindu mind".

Look at the "dowry deaths", burning of young wives daily reported in their own media. To which caste they belong? They are mostly upper castes. Keep a cutting of all these reports published in their own toilet papers. Why these Hindus are burning and killing their own women? Why they are persisting with *sati*, widow-burning, female foeticide? Why do they get a vicarious pleasure in this violence? The cause is this twist in the "Hindu mind" which is threatening the country's unity and integrity. ■

----

8 - Cricket as India's national religion

Our Brahminical boasting brats will not stop boasting even after India ate dust in the Sydney Olympic Games. What a shame. Not merely in sports, even in economic development, health or education India has been always at the bottom of the pit. But this did not stop of our boasting brats.

Boasting is the "national character" of these brats. If they get the No.1 position in anything in the world it is in boasting. None can surpass them in boasting. If there is an international boasting competition our Brahminical heroes will get all the gold.

What is the reason for this peculiar disease afflicting India? No. India as a whole is not suffering from this boasting disease. This disease is confined only to the ruling class comprising a mere 15% of the population. We have coined a name for this class — Brahminical Social Order (BSO)— a name which has now become famous.

Beijing Olympics

The rest of the population is pure. A dark-skinned woman, Karnam Malleswari, a Telugu Backward Caste woman who alone saved India's little remaining honour by securing a Bronze, belonged to this non-BSO Bahujan majority class. If our beef-eating Dalit and tribal boys and girls with their extraordinary stamina had been selected to the Olympics, they would have brought more gold and greater glory. But the Brahminical boasting brats will not allow our dark-looking boys and girls to come up. They want only the Aryan grass-eating, fair-skinned, pot-bellied guys who are good only at boasting. So, in Sydney they rightly ate dust. But the BSO has no regret. No shame. The Beijing Olympics is coming up in 2008. You can test the truth of this statement.

Here lies the peculiar psyche of the BSO. We call it the "Hindu mind". Why the BSO is not interested in India achieving glory? Why our great "nationalist", "patriotic", *Bharat Mata*-worshipping Brahminical boasting brats are anti-national? Why they don't love India? Why they are not proud of their land?

We will get the answer to this question if we study the twist in the "Hindu mind". The ruling BSO is not interested in keeping India's flag flying high either at the Olympics or anywhere else. They are interested only in enjoying. But enjoying at other's cost.

World famous beggar

India has become a world famous beggar country. There is no country in the world from which BSO has not borrowed. But such a beggar had sent one of the biggest teams to Sydney. (In 1982, when the Asiad Games was staged in Delhi India's rank was 115 out of the 150 countries in the world). Why? It is not to win and bring honour to India but such a big team of BSO members was sent to Sydney but to enjoy. Every action of the BSO is taken exclusively from the point of view of bringing enjoyment to its members.

As long as we keep this tiny, parasitic Brahminical class as our rulers, India will not only continue as beggar but bring not merely shame but disaster after disaster to the country in all fronts including Olympics. As the BSO is having its monopoly media to control our minds, it is able to shift the entire blame on Pakistani ISI or some "deadly terrorists".

For these Brahminical boasting brats the most ideal game is

cricket, which has become our new "national" religion. But the problem is this "game of idlers" is considered neither a game nor a sport. That is why cricket is not admitted to the Olympics.

Cricket is neither a man nor a woman. It is a eunuch. No modern industrialised country can afford to play this "game of idlers" which Bernard Shaw once famously ridiculed as a silly sport in which "11 fools play and 11,000 fools watch".

Powerful uniting factor

Except Britain, no powerful and busy country plays cricket. Because they don't want to waste their precious time. But even in Britain, cricket is not their national game. It is football. But the BSO has plenty of leisure and tons of ill-earned income. For such lazy lizards cricket is the ideal game and hence rightly it is elevated to the status of a new "national" religion which has greater emotional pull and push than the BSO's newly assembled "religion" called hotchpotch Hinduism. At least Christians and Muslims may tend to disagree on this hotchpotch Hinduism but show us one dissenting *nastik* before the god of cricket. Involuntarily and unthinkingly a feeling of oneness is created by this stupid game called cricket. Yes, it is cricket that creates "one India". Hence the religion of cricket is a more powerful uniting factor than their hotchpotch Hinduism.

Not even the latest discovery of massive corruption in cricket and the income tax crack down on cricketers will diminish the power of this "national" religion. Corruption is the core of BSO. This BSO became the ruling class only through corruption of all varieties — caste corruption, moral corruption, money corruption. And the most serious intellectual corruption. (*India's Intellectual Desert*, DSA-1999).

So, even if all the cricketers are hauled up nothing will happen to them because both the cricketers and the powerful cricket lobby behind them belong to the BSO. They are the rulers. Who can punish the rulers? It is the rulers who will punish others.

Corruption in cricket

Look at Jaya Jetly, a Malayali upper caste woman once heading a Backward Caste Kurmi Party (Samata), defending the cricketer's right to be corrupt. She called a press conference in her friend, the then Defence Minister George Fernandes' official residence in Delhi to denounce the income tax authorities for doing their duty against her daughter, a girl friend of cricketer Ajay Jadeja, hauled up by the tax people. All this shows that not even a mouse will be killed in the *hangama* kicked up by the fraud called match-fixing.

Cricket forms the most important ingredient of the entertainment-packed menu of the rulers who themselves are buried under mountains of corruption and became rulers because of corruption.

That means the match-fixing corruption scandal raised in the media is yet another entertainment to keep this chatter-box leisured class entertained. Whole thing is a farce.

Which corrupt fellow has been sent to gallows in India? In China, recently a very high-ranking communist party functionary was convicted on corruption, sentenced to death and quickly executed. That is China. And that is how China is on the top of the world and came No.2 in the Sydney Olympics. India came last. Yet we have no shame. Our "national pride" is not hurt. When the Brahminical boasting brats returned from Sydney there was no black flag or rotten eggs thrown to greet them. This is India.

Dark-skinned Dravidas

In population China stands No.1 in the world and India No.2. But China maintains its lead in all spheres — including human development. But India only boasts and our human development is utterly neglected. Nay. Human beings in India are treated worse than worms. The BSO is worried only about the 15% Aryans. The rest of the 85% dark-skinned Dravidas (Bahujans) do not matter. It is a clear division.

How can we expect a set of idiotic drones, who spend days and days discussing the silly cricket, to come up in sports and games? They will neither allow the sturdy Dalits and Tribals to come up nor will they encourage any powerful sport or games.

Cricket has destroyed all our sporting talent. The extraordinary media attention and glamour bestowed on the over-pampered corrupt cricketers has demoralised all other sports and games. None of our game or sport will come up as long as cricket is held as our "national" religion — a game tailor-made to this leisured class.

Population as an asset

Our world famous boasting brats claim that India houses the largest reservoir of intellectual talent in the world. We know the capacity of the BSO to make false claims. When the then Soviet Russia sent the first man to moon, the *papans* sitting for their daily evening gossip at Mylapore (Madras) boasted that India had conquered the moon (*chandra loka*) centuries before the Russians did it. Such is our capacity for boasting.

But these boasting brats who claim that they possess the best brains in the world do not have that much of brain that development of sports and games cannot be achieved in isolation. You can't develop any sports neglecting human development. China, which has the world's largest population, made use of this great asset and every individual is recognized and respected. That is how China is able to come No.2 at the Olympics. Soon it will be No.1 beating even the USA. China will be No.1 not only in sports and games, it will be No.1 in every field. It will be the 21st century's No.1 country.

Why? Because China puts its great asset of population to the best use while the BSO rulers hate its people and do their best to destroy them — through population control. This is the difference. We had been to China twice (before our passport was impounded in 1986) and we have seen with our own eyes the great achievements of China. But the BSO braggarts dismiss China as a "communist" country with no democracy. But their own hero, Jayaprakash Narayan (JP), had said China had better democracy than India where we have only one freedom — the freedom to starve, freedom to remain as slaves. And the freedom to die — that too without peace.

Killing Ravana & Bali

Sports and games can develop only in a nation-state where all its citizens are brothers and sisters. How can any camaraderie develop in India where the greatest heroes of Bahujans are ridiculed and burnt as evil incarnate in officially sponsored festivals? In *Ram Lila* our greatest hero Ravana is being burnt every year. In *Dipavali* our most respected ancestor, Bali Chakravarti, is also burnt. Ravana and Bali are remembered, loved and respected in each and every corner of India. But have we protested the Hindu fury on our heroes?

We cannot. We have no right to find fault with the BSO because it is we the Bahujans who installed this BSO as our rulers. And they are ruling us. Rulers do not go wrong. Are the aggrieved, cheated, enslaved, dehumanised Bahujans getting angry?

Until we get angry and smash this tiny criminal gang, India will continue to be a beggar nation, a laughing stock of the whole world.

But the BSO does not care whether the world laughs or weeps over this sick "nation" as long as it remains as the ruling class.

The problem is not the BSO rulers. The problem is our own Bahujans who have not even identified this enemy oppressor. There lies the beauty and the strength of BSO. ■

----

9 – The Hindu belief system

The Hindu belief system (faith) is not like the other faiths in the world like Islam, Christianity, Budhism, Sikhism or any other religion. The Hindu belief system has taken hold of the very brain of the Hindu and reduced him to an unthinking moron. India, they say, is world famous for its "spiritualism" but spiritualism in India has an entirely different meaning by which the Brahminical rulers dictate things to their advantage and call it spiritualism.

No other country has so many "spiritual leaders" as in India. "Spiritual" need not necessarily mean religious. One can be spiritual without being religious. Spiritualism has nothing to do with god or religion. Dr. Babasaheb Ambedkar, the Father of India, was spiritual but he was not religious. India has a special meaning for spirituality. Our saffron-clad *swamis* (godmen) are its custodians holding the neck of the masses of India. They say India has its own unique spirituality. What they mean is the Brahminical rituals and blind faith which brings the Brahmins all the income. In other words spirituality is linked to regular income to the godmen. Palmistry, meditation, astrology, serpent worship, "holy" river bath (*kumbh mela*), temple visit, blind belief in the holy scriptures and the words of holy men —all these are part of the faith which are not to be questioned. Spirituality is claimed as the special genius of Hindu India.

Even the highest court of India has no courage to deliberate on faith. So much so this blind faith has caused so much damage to the country's education system, public life and the very future of the country. Neither during the 1,000 year Budhist rule, 800-year Muslim rule nor during the 200-year British rule they could interfere with the country's Hindu belief system. They say Hinduism is the world's oldest religion. But they don't know that there is nothing like Hinduism. India's Supreme Court itself said it is not a religion but a way of life. Every other religion has a founder, a core philosophy, a religious text and a god. Hinduism has nothing of this. For details read Arun Shourie's book, *Hinduism: Essence & Consequence* (Vikas, New Delhi).

Even M.K. Gandhi, who throughout his life dabbled in politics, is called a spiritual guru. But the problem with all these spiritual leaders is none of them was able to liberate India and take it to higher level and make it a modern state to compete with the best of the world. All its Hindu spiritual wisdom could not liberate the Hindu himself from slavery and beggar mentality. Even a Western-educated Brahmin nuclear scientist suffers from all sorts of superstitions and calls it his faith.

None can purify Ganga waters

The best example of Indian spirituality is reflected in the country's "holiest" river Ganga. The belief is a dip in it will take you straight to heaven. But one should go to the Ganga and see its water — fully contaminated with dead bodies floating. The French Government was given the contract to clean the Ganga. After trying for some years it gave up saying that none can purify the Ganga. India's spiritualism is exactly like the Ganga water.

Hindu religion is a pure business putting on a garb of spiritualism. It is also a mixture of so many tempting things to make it a saleable commodity: sex, entertainment, intoxication and of course a dose of spirituality.

Holy people (*swamis*) have a huge following. Mata Amritananda Mayi, is a dark-skinned, uneducated fisher woman from the west-coast Kerala State, groomed by the Hindu terrorist political party to instigate clashes between fishermen and Muslims who together do the fishing business in the Kerala coast. She is given wide publicity in the country's Brahminical monopoly media and told that she possessed great spiritual power and the poor, gullible people are made to believe it. They flock in millions and pour their hard-earned money which go into the coffers of the Hindu terrorist parties to terrorise Muslims and Christians on one side and *hinduise* (enslave) the non-Hindu Untouchables and Tribals. Called *Amma,* her most famous gift is for hugging. That is all. People Q up in thousands to be hugged by her. The propaganda is she has so far hugged 30 million people. We don't know who keeps a count of her hugging.

Who is the founder of this great, ancient religion? Nobody knows. What is its central philosophy? Nobody knows. Each *swami* has his own interpretation of Hinduism which has almost become a global enterprise. Amma's foundation runs branches in 30 countries. Most of the money goes for the benefit of the Hindu terrorist party.

Satya Sai Baba

As the Indian ruling Brahminical people, who have a strong presence in USA, started joining hands with the American Jews who control that country's economy, media, administration and even its Christian church, there has been a steady flow of Indian "holy men" into USA and their influence is growing. The Jews and Brahmins having come together to fight their common enemy of Muslims, the *swamis* of India have before them a very flourishing market in USA and West in general.

Satya Sai Baba, India's richest godman, is a Telugu speaker

belonging to a Backward Caste Raju *jati*. He knows no other language other than his mother tongue though he is called *Bhagwan* (god). But the Hindu belief system has made the Hindu so blind that they can't think that the god is omniscient. At least he should know all the languages. But the Sai Baba knows no other language except Telugu. But the Hindu believes what he wants to believe.

If Satya Sai Baba is god why he is complaining that he is ageing and suffering from several ailments? Why he has to be lifted always? The Hindu mind is blind to all these. It never questions. The "Hindu mind" means blind belief.

Hinduism is anti-science

The Hindu belief system kills the very thinking power in a person. That is why India has not produced any outstanding scientist or original thinker except Dr. Babasaheb Ambedkar who was not a Hindu but anti-Hindu.

Scientific research has no takers. No industrial unit has any R&D Dept. Hinduism is essentially anti-science. Growth of science is possible if there are questioning minds. But Hinduism says its tenets can't be questioned. You have to blindly believe. How can science grow in such an atmosphere?

If Satya Sai Baba is a god why he "materialises" only ring, ash and things like that for his rich devotees? Why can't he "materialise" food for the starving millions? Till today no Hindu scientist has questioned this.

But the Hindu has a quick stock answer. He says the god cannot save the poor. The poor are starving because they are destined to starve. That is what is written on the foreheads of the poor. They have committed lot of sins in their previous birth and hence they are destined to suffer. It was god's punishment. How can the god save those whom he has himself cursed? Wonderful logic.

In other words, the Hindu gods are there to bless only the rich and the powerful.

What about the allegations of homosexuality against the Satya Sai Baba? An Australian victim had written a book itself in English and had presented a copy of it to us (We have since lost it).

But his devotees won't believe any of these. For them he is the god. What this god has done to the people? The quick answer is he has built hospitals and colleges. But many monied people have also built such things to make more money and the Baba is doing nothing more. Can we say all these monied people are also god?

Homo-sexuality charge

The Hindu belief system will never promote a questioning mind.

You tell them about the homo-sexuality charge. Google has 18,000 references on Sai Baba's homosexual adventures. Most of the complaints are from Westerners. Indians will never complain and if he has a complaint, he will be called mad.

Senior "scientists" are his devotees. The Indian Institute of Science, Bangalore, the country's apex scientific institution which has an international reputation, once invited the Sai Baba to speak on "science and spiritualism". The intention is to kill the little remaining science in India. This writer was present in that session and when a person from the audience raised the charge of homosexuality against Sai Baba he was pushed out. Scientists in India are also Hindu and have a "Hindu mind" —not a scientific mind.

Such an idiotic behaviour of Hindus can be well judged when

India's presidents, prime ministers, chief justices and army chiefs fall on his feet. Which police will have the courage to file a case against the Sai Baba who is accused of murdering six people in his own bed room at Puttaparti, his headquarters, when such VVIPs fall on his feet in public?

Sai Baba's "miracles" are another big hoax. Sri Lanka's Rationalist, the late Abraham Kovoor, and Calcutta's famous magician P.C. Sorcar have called the bluff. But the Hindu will not believe all this. The Hindu belief system will not make him think.

Sai Baba can "materialise" only such things which he can hold within his fist. Nothing bigger. He can't present you a water melon. But he can give you expensive watches, rings, ash and things like which he can hide inside his palm.

Yes. Alright he can do some "miracles" like this. All magicians also do it. They also produce a rabbit. But Sai Baba has never done it. They even cut a live girl and separate her head and you can see the blood flowing. The next minute the girl comes out alive. The magician says it is mass hypnotism. He doesn't say it is a miracle and that he has godly powers.

Vice-Chancellor dismissed

But Sai Baba is not doing hypnotism. He is god himself. To that extent we have become duds. Even top scientists do not question him.

Over decades back this writer was part of a miracle-investigation team headed by the then Vice-Chancellor of Bangalore University, Dr. H. Narasimhaiah. The entire Brahminical lot revolted against the un-Hindu activity of Dr. Narasimhiah and he was dismissed. Anybody criticising Sai Baba is finished. Dead. Such is the power of this god and the Brahminical myth-makers.

P.C. Sorcar once went to Sai Baba's *Ashram* in Bangalore and was booted out by his goons for producing ash, ring and a wrist watch much better than Sai Baba. Sorcar wrote an article in the then Calcutta journal, *Sunday*.

The Hindu belief system attributes great healing power to the Sai Baba. If he is "healing" others why he built hospitals? Can't he "heal" them instead of employing doctors in such expensive hospitals he has built? If you put this question, the "Hindu mind" gets irritated and there is a chance of your being dubbed anti-Hindu.

If Sai Baba can predict the future, why he could not anticipate the two assassination attempts on his own life? He could not even change the Google which called him a "sick mind".

He is getting billions and billions of rupees from the sick minds of India who have made money through all illegal mean. That money he is investing in "charity" which is so widely advertised. For that he can at best be called a philanthropist. Not god. Rama Krishna Mission has done much bigger philanthropy. So also Mother Teresa. Nobody has claimed that he is god.

Satya Sai Baba is a rich man's god. We can hardly find any poor going to see him. They have no entry. The people of his own village, Puttaparti, his own *jatwalas* hate him. They say he has spoiled the peace of the village. ■

DV Sept.1, 2005 p.8: "A poor magician called Satya Sai Baba".

DV July 16, 2004 p.6: "Sodomy charges against Sai Baba: Havoc of godman".

DV Feb.16, 2002 p.11: "Is it possible to kill god?"

DV Jan.16, 1994 p.5: "Sai Baba murder case takes new turn".

DV July 16, 1993: "Truth about Baba and his blacksheep".

DV Oct.1, 1982 p. 10: "Sue Satya Sai Baba for sodomy".

----

10 – World's most violent country

Karl Marx said religion is the opium of masses. If you want to verify the truth of this statement, please come to India to witness how the so-called reigning religion of the land is drugging its masses and keeping them in eternal thrall. There are some countries till having slavery. But India is not only having slaves but slaves enjoying their slavery. Not only it has 330 million gods and goddesses but almost every village of Hindu India has its own godmen (called *swami* or *guru*) who are more powerful than the god himself.

"Sri Sri Sri" Ravi Shankar, a Bangalore Brahmin, has become the latest craze of the affluent class. Being a Brahmin he naturally gets lots of media build-up and all sorts of concocted stories are built round him to make him a cult figure and finally replace the dying Satya Sai Baba. His Bangalore *Ashram* has assets worth billions of dollars. The only thing he specialises is in meditation which itself is as old as Hinduism.

However, he did not "discover" meditation which every *swami* does and yet Ravi Shankar is given all the credit for meditation, which has become the craze for the upper caste elite. Meditation has become the food of the affluent who after making money through all sorts of illegal ways easily fall a prey to such tricksters like Ravi Shankar. Meditation is no cure but the Hindu belief system makes you believe anything and everything the *guru* says.

His "Art of Living" (AOL) is nothing but the fine Art of Deceiving in which he is an expert. That is how AOL has become a super rich Brahminical institution.

There are millions *swamis* and *gurus* in this mad, mad world called

Hindu India. We need a whole book itself to write on these thugs that dot the length and breadth of India.

But all these *swamis* and *gurus* put together have not reduced the rampant corruption in which India is buried neck deep. Nor India's shocking poverty and deprivation. All those who run to these swamis are mostly the rich who invariably are also corrupt because it is not possible in a very poor country like India to become rich without cheating, bribing and stealing.

There is one at Mysore city who is said to be keeping the enormous money of the late Prime Minister P.V. Narasimha Rao. Both are Telugu Brahmins. This postman-turned swami is the favourite of politicians to keep their secret funds. Neither the income tax nor the police can enter their *ashrams* because they themselves are corrupt and all corrupt will have to become devotees of such *swamis* to cover up their sins.

World's only religion of non-violence

Hinduism is advertised all over the world as the world's only religion which stands for non-violence (*ahimsa*) but no country in the world is as violent as India. In fact, Hinduism is the world's most violent "religion". If India is so "spiritually rich" and this spirituality is built on the foundation of tolerance, why the country has daily religious bloodbath in one part or other?

The quick answer is the politicians are exploiting the Hindu religion. But the fact is the Hindu terrorist party of RSS-BJP has formed a council of all Hindu religious leaders (*swamis*) called "Vishwa Hindu Parishad" (VHP) which is behind all attacks on Christian, Muslim and Sikhs. Wherever bloodbath begins, the VHP is always involved. The Hindu terrorist party came to power only by killing Muslims. And yet the claim is Hinduism stands for non-violence.

The double-speak of the Brahminical leadership of the Hindu is they swear by "tolerance" but in the same breath they cry for the blood of Muslims forming 20% of the country's population. All the central items on the RSS-BJP agenda is directed against Muslim and Christian: such as ban on cow slaughter, ban on conversion, uniform civil code, building Ram temple on a Muslim masjid in UP. The moment a Hindu leader opens his mouth we can see him breathing fire against Muslims. The birth of "Hindu India" was by spilling the blood of thousands of Muslims in partition riots. The 1947 partition of India was a cunning Brahminical device blessed by M.K. Gandhi, the Father of the (Hindu) Nation, to pack off the Muslims, coming in the way of Brahmin takeover of India, to a separate country.

Babri Masjid demolition

Hindu terrorist party RSS is a hydra-headed serpent and its agenda is nothing but hate-mongering through and through. It has nothing positive, nothing constructive. What it says is if India becomes a *Hindu Rashtra,* meaning Hindu nation, all its problems get automatically solved in one breath. But in very next breath it says 85% of India's people are Hindu. How a minuscule of 15% non-Hindus can undo the "nation" of 85% Hindu? There is no answer. They go on heaping abuses on Muslims and Christians. If the 85% Indians are Hindu, why it is keeping 15% of its Untouchables as slaves who are also called Hindu? There is no answer. A Hindu believes what he wants to believe.

Even after 16 years of demolishing the 16th century Muslim (Babri) masjid claiming it to be the birth place of their god Ram, they have not been able to build a temple for their god. The demolition of the masjid itself was a conspiracy of a Brahmin Prime Minister of the Congress Party and the entire Brahminical people on the question, including its Supreme Court, on preserving and perpetuating their Brahminical religion. Brahmins and other upper castes in every party have one opinion on this subject that the Muslims have to live at the mercy of Hindus. If so how then can they call India a democracy? A democracy assures equal rights to every citizen but under the Hindu democracy those against Brahminism have no right. They have to be at the mercy of the rulers.

The country right from its independence (1947) was ruled by only Brahminical people. Most of the Prime Ministers were Brahmins. But as years pass the country is drifting aimlessly. ■

----

11 — Where are the *Deshbhaktas*?

Very often India's Hindu terrorist RSS party leaders declare themselves as the greatest *Deshbhaktas* (patriots) and malign Muslims as traitors and terrorists and call them anti-nationals. What they mean by this is Hindus (15% upper castes) alone are patriots and the rest including the indigenous SC/ST/BCs are not.

As the Hindus are holding the neck of the country and have their hand-picked men and women in the media, they can say anything and get away with it. In fact they have impressed even the entire world itself about their patriotism, the greatness of their non-violence, their devotion to justice and truth. Paragon of all virtues. Fine. But actually is the fact?

Dr. Babasaheb Ambedkar, the Father of India, had to write a book itself, *What Congress and Gandhi Have Done to Untouchables?* (1945, pp.380, Thacker & Co. Ltd., Bombay) to refute all the Hindu allegations made by M.K. Gandhi, a third-ranking Hindu, who did so much for the Brahmins and to secure world-wide publicity for the "Hindu services" to the Untouchables. But the pity is after fully using the services of the Gujarati Bania, Gandhi was finally assassinated by a Hindu (a Brahmin) only. We have written a book itself on this subject, *Why Godse Killed Gandhi?* (DSA-1997). Gandhi who handed over the country to Hindus by deceiving the Muslims, Sikhs and Untouchables was not killed by any of his victims but by a hard-core Brahmin belonging to the very same Hindu terrorist party RSS which alone claims the credit for *Deshbhakti* (patriotism).

What happened to these *Deshbhaktas* now in the year 2008 (61 years after the country's "independence") when the country's army chief himself expressed shock over the crippling shortage of 11,5000 officers? India's 1.13-million strong army is facing such a serious problem that no *Deshbhakta* is coming forward to offer his services in defence of his beloved land. Why? The Hindu propaganda is they alone are the patriots and Muslim, Sikh, Christian are anti-national and the rest (SC/ST/BCs -65%) are useless. Only the Hindus (15%) are the genuine lovers of the land. *Deshbhaktas*.

Sikhs kept out of Army

Already the country's defence services are in a very bad shape. Much of the men and material are committed to defend the "disputed" Kashmir on which several wars were fought. In the East and the North, China is "occupying" a huge chunk of our land for the past several decades. The *Deshbhaktas* in love with their land should have fought the Chinese and recovered the land under their occupation. They did not do it because they dare not do it. At least they should have volunteered to join the army and other wings of defence services. But they are not coming. At the same time they shout from their house top that *Deshbhakti* is their sole prerogative and daily tease and taunt us for being anti-national. They are finding fault mainly with Muslims and even SC/ST/BCs. Even the percentage of Sikhs — called the gate-keepers of India who once dominated the defence services and displayed extraordinary courage and laid down their lives in defence of the mother land — in the army has simply come down after the "Blue Star Operation (1985) suspecting their loyalty to the "mother land". Muslims are hardly found as they are also added to the list of terrorists.

When the country is "threatened" by Pakistan on one side and China on the other, why our *Deshbhaktas* having kept out Muslims and Sikhs as traitors are not coming forward to join the army?

Conscription

The Army Chief, Deepak Kapoor, a Punjabi upper caste Hindu, has become so desperate that for the first time in the history of the country he hinted at conscription — compulsory military service which is there in America where the upper castes (Hindus) have their heart.

The army is facing double trouble. It is facing haemorrhage on two sides. New Hindu recruits to commissioned officer posts are not coming and those Hindus already occupying top positions in the army are threatening to quit. Press reports on April 15, 2008 said 65 Army officers have put in their papers following the Fifth Pay Commission Report which did not treat them on par with civil service (IAS) officers.

The Indian Army is almost 100% upper caste monopoly because the Muslims and Sikhs, the two martial races, have been unofficially declared anti-national and kept out. But at the non-commissioned level of *jawans* (soldiers) it is fully non-Hindu, divided into caste-based regiments. It is these low-paid *jawans* who actually do the donkey's duty on the freezing Himalayan heights and other fighting fronts. The *jawans* are not permitted to take their family into the barracks. But the *Deshbhakta* Hindu officers live in right royal luxury with their family in large bungalows and enjoying all the facilities.

The upper castes will not miss a single opportunity to declare their *Deshbhakti* but when army chief Deepak Kapoor hinted at compulsory military duty he was shouted down by his own Hindus. The Hindu howl was so loud that the Govt. of India itself had to deny any plan for conscription. What happened to our *Deshbhaktas*?

World's largest illiterate country

India has turned into world's largest illiterate country as our upper caste rulers have deliberately kept the "low caste" SC/ST/BCs out of school. This is because the Hindus alone have the right to education and that too higher education. In other words only the 15% upper castes can get into commissioned posts.

This puts a question mark on their *Deshbhakti*. Their argument is defence services are not attractive. IT and such other "soft jobs" are not only high paid but involves less physical labour and high risks. Brahmins being mostly vegetarians are incapable of doing hard work. That is why they opt for "soft job" which involves mostly manipulative work. That is why nobody is entering the defence services.

Then who should defend the "motherland" and die for *Deshbhakti*? Why can't the RSS, which sells "patriotism" to us, send its own boys to join the army ?

Dalits died in hundreds in the 1999 Kargil War but the Hindus had no appreciation for their suffering and sacrifice.

America, Israel (with which the Brahminical rulers are having close ties and even secret defence pacts), France and many other countries have conscription. No youth can get a degree unless he has compulsorily served the defence forces.

The Kargil war revealed that most of the people who died in this latest war with Pakistan were the low caste SC/ST/BCs. But none praised them because the Hindu sympathy goes only to their *jatwalas*. But why should it be the sole duty of the despised low castes to die on the war front when the upper castes claim all the credit for the *Deshbhakti*? The upper caste argument is the low castes opt for army services because of their poverty and once recruited to army they have to compulsorily serve on the war front and die. Why should anybody call it *Deshbhakti* when they did not die to display their patriotism but out of necessity? The Hindu alone is capable of such strange arguments. In Hindu India the poor (SC/ST/BCs are the country's poorest) only die unsung and unwept whether during the war or peace.

The only way to compel the rich (meaning the upper castes) is conscription which will force them to bear the pain or share the pain so far exclusively reserved for the non-Hindu SC/ST/BCs.

Army chief made to shut up

If you want the *Deshbhakti* to be forced on these *Idli-Sambar* cowards, the burden of dying should be forced upon all. Every able bodied Indian should suffer and die to exhibit his *Deshbhakti*. Debar the country's able bodied youth to receive the degree if he does not serve the defence services compulsorily. At least one year he has to be a frontline soldier. Are the *Deshbhaktas* ready?

No. Deepak Kapoor was simply made to shut up and the Govt. of India itself denied any move for conscription which died even before it was born.

Where is the patriotism of our upper caste drones?

The Hindu talk of *Deshbhakti* is only to slander the country's three religious "minorities" — Muslim, Christian and Sikh — together forming about 20% of the population. As the ruling upper castes have also kept out the SC/ST/BCs, the non-Hindu indigenous, from the commissioned posts in the three defences services, thy want to prove through such a propaganda that only the Hindus as the genuine *Deshbhaktas* and the rest are *Deshadrohis* (traitors).

But the facts put out by the Govt. of India and the Army chief do not prove the *Deshbhakti* of the Hindu grass-eaters.

Parasurama killed all Kshatriyas

The Hindus by nature are not given to hard work. They are essentially pleasure-lovers. That is how India has one of the highest number of holidays a year. They are still not happy — want more and more holidays to lead their life of pomp and pleasure. Of the four castes that comprise the upper castes — the Brahmin, Kshatriya, Vaishya and *shudra*— only the Kshatriyas have been the martial race but the Brahmin god, Parashurama, killed all of them. Those calling themselves today Thakurs and Rajputs may be those Kshatriyas though their population strength is very poor.

The Brahmins and Vaishyas are normally manipulators and genetically first class cowards being grass-eaters. Brahmins in particular are plenty in the top defence posts but occupying decorative positions leaving the hard and risky job of fighting to the *jawans*. Except for the northern borders, the country as a whole has never witnessed any large-scale warfare. The army, navy and air force officer posts are occupied by the upper castes and even they are quitting opting for kushy jobs in the private sector. Why these Hindus, who ridicule Muslims and Sikhs as anti-national, are not thinking of the country's interests? Where is their *Deshbhakti*?

The following *Times of India* report of Jan.1, 2008 makes an alarming reading:

> **New Delhi:** The latest statistics show the Army is grappling with a shortage of 11,238 officers in an "authorized" strength of 46,615. To top that, around 3,000 offices have applied for premature retirement just since 2004.
>
> What's making the situation alarming is the fact that in both the entry-level institutions of the Army — the National Defence Academy, Khadakwasla, and Indian Military Academy, Dehra Dun — there was a sharp decline in youngsters queuing up to join this year.
>
> The NDA, for instance, has a course vacancy of 300, but only 190 of the selected cadets joined this year. Things are even worse at IMA, with only 86 "gentlemen cadets" joining for a course vacancy of 250. "It's fact. We are not getting the right material.. The corporate world pays much more than what the government and the armed forces can give. Young men find emoluments much better outside. It has become a big source of worry since we do not wish to lower our quality standards", admitted Gen. Deepak Kapoor.

The report makes it clear that the upper castes are driven by their love for money — not *Deshbhakti*.

Who is migrating to West?

If the corporate world pays more and hence attractive, who will defend the country? They are not worried. The upper caste rulers do not trust the Muslims and Sikhs, both declared untrustworthy for "sensitive posts" in Defence Services. The upper caste youth want to study in India but run away to West cursing the country for not giving them good salary. Medical doctors and management (IIM graduates) grandees say the salary scales in

India are so "unattractive" that they are forced to migrate to the West. Good argument.

Then who is going to defend India? Love of the motherland means you have to serve sacrificing everything. But the upper castes are not ready to sacrifice even a single pleasure. Then to whom are they teaching *Deshbhakti*?

Muslims and Sikhs in particular have plenty of youths ready to enter the military academies and serve the defence forces but they are kept out. The upper castes complaining poor pay are not entering defence services. Then who will defend India?

Where are our *Deshbhaktas*? ■

----

12 – Why Hindu India will not have a revolution ?

The urban, educated upper castes (Hindu) get irritated if anybody talks of caste. Having gone up the ladder solely on the strength of his caste, he now wants to hide his caste. When he can't hide the caste which now and then raises its ugly head, he naturally loses his temper and hits back saying "where is caste?" But the fact is the urban educated Hindu is the most caste conscious. The entire IT industry is the monopoly of the Brahmins and other upper castes. All professions — medical, engineering, accountants, legal, banking, trade, commerce and industry, media etc. — are also the monopoly of the upper castes and yet he asks "where is caste?" But it does not occur to this bigoted Hindu that caste continues only through marriage and the matrimonial columns in top English dailies carry columns and columns of advertisement, all from our upper caste, highly educated, foreign-returned fellows seeking a pretty, educated girl of his own caste. Marriage within the caste perpetuates caste. The highly educated Hindu who becomes furious when anybody raises caste, lives within his caste, his caste laws and performs all his caste duties even while he does not like to admit the existence of caste — because his wounded psyche suddenly gets dipped in chilly powder and suffers unbearable pain. His conscience pricks when caste is mentioned. That is why he gets annoyed.

How then the "educated Hindu" is all shocked when we say caste is still reigning supreme? This proves that even our highly educated Hindus have not developed the power of thinking. Thinking and Hinduism cannot go together. Such is the power of Hinduism.

Does Hinduism recognise liberty? Even after 61 years of "independence", over 50% of our population remains illiterate. How did the Hindu rulers deprive the liberty of the people to get education? Free, compulsory and universal primary education is provided in the constitution but the *Manu Dharma*, the Hindu constitution, prevailed over the constitution made by Dr. B.R. Ambedkar.

Hinduism denies freedom of vocation. Even today all over India, in all municipal towns, the sweepers and scavengers are Untouchables. You can't choose your job. The job of a temple priest is exclusively reserved for the Brahmin. There is caste even within the army with its caste-based regiments. Your job is fixed under Hinduism. That is how Hindu India has become the world's largest illiterate country.

Killer Modi glorified

Does Hinduism recognise fraternity — which is the other name for fellow-feeling? When Chief Minister Narendra Modi, killed over 2,000 Muslims in cold blood in the famous "Gujarat Genocide-2002" did the Hindus weep? No. The upper castes rejoiced. The rest of the Hindus were indifferent.

Marxism failed in Hindu India because the Hindus have no fellow-feeling. Hindus don't like to suffer even with the suffering Hindus. That is how "caste wars" have become so frequent in India. Killing of Christians, Muslims, Sikhs make the Hindu a hero. Narendra Modi is one such "hero" created by Hindus. In case some Hindus get shocked Hindu newspapers mislead the people by dubbing them "terrorists", a tag which permits the govt. itself to recklessly use state force to kill Muslim, Christian, Sikh and naxalites.

That is how India has turned into one of the world's most violent countries. The Brahmin Parasurama, who killed the entire Kshatriyas, is the guru of the Chitpavan Brahmins. In the hundreds of "caste wars" the state itself takes sides. Where is the fraternity under Hinduism? Where is the sharing and caring? When there is a train accident and scores lay dead or injured, the people on the spot rarely rush for medicare or relief. They are more interested in stealing whatever they get. When a cyclone battered the east coast and hundreds lay dead, the govt. could not find people to clear the bodies. Because they did not know which caste the dead belonged. The Missionaries of Charity of the Mother Teresa rushed from Calcutta and cleared the dead. The same was the experience during the Tsunami on the Tamil Nadu coastline. Muslim, Christian and Sikhs run charity mission. But there is no such thing like Hindu charity. A Hindu at least may share a thing with his caste man. Not an outsider. The sentiment of fraternity is foreign to Hindu.

Preaching hatred

Because his religion did not teach him sharing and caring. A Hindu will not inter-marry or inter-dine. Exceptions only go to prove the rule. Under Hinduism there is nothing like fraternity. Inequality and hatred are the religious doctrines of the Hindu. No big Hindu temple runs any hospital. The income is used exclusively for the Brahmins who run it.

Every Hindu scripture preaches only man's inequality to man. The Vedas preach the *Chaturvarna* and M.K. Gandhi's favourite *Bhagawad Gita* is *Manu Dharma Sastra* in nutshell. And the Brahmins were the authors of these texts preaching inequality and hatred.

Dr. Babasaheb Ambedkar said:

"Hinduism, thy name is inequality" and "Inequality is the soul of Hinduism". (Dr. Ambedkar, *W&S*, Vol.3, 1987, p.87).

Hindus give so much of importance to "merit". But this is just to malign the constitutional provisions giving reservation to Dalits, Backwards etc. (V.T. Rajshekar, *Merit, My Foot*, DSA-2006). When the Hindus do not recognise fraternity how can they recognise merit? To them merit is confined only to their *jati*.

Dr. Ambedkar asked the Hindus to destroy their caste system so that there could be a level playing field for all the castes. But the Hindus not only rejected his plea but withdrew the invitation to deliver a lecture on this subject at Lahore in the pre-independent India.

"To each according to his needs and from each according to his ability" is the marxist principle. The Hindu principle is from each according to his need and to each according to his nobility. That is how even to this day the caste system is in tact, deathless.

Worship of superman

A Brahmin, Nathuram Godse, might have killed M.K. Gandhi but it was the same Brahmins who elevated him to the highest level of "Father of the nation" and called him a *Mahatma*. This is as per the most striking feature of Hinduism: the worship of the superman. This superman has no duty towards the suffering humans. But it is his duty to collect charity from anybody and everybody. Every class of citizens has to serve this superman, who is none other than the Brahmin.

The oppressed people have no right to rise, not even the right to protest. You have every right to do anything you want except questioning the Brahminical Social Order. Because the BSO is a divine order designed by the god himself. Whose god? Of course the Brahmin god who is also the servant of the Brahmin. Hindus are the only people in the world where their social order is made by god himself and hence cannot be questioned and so will remain permanent and eternal. True to its dictates, ever since the Brahmin forged this social order, it has remained permanent — deathless without even a change of a coma. How then can there be a revolution in India?

When Budhism, which was the first to question the Brahminical Social Order, came the Brahmins conspired and killed it. When Budhism could survive in the whole of East Asia how in India alone it died? How even the very memory of Budha is erased out of the memory of our people? Look, how efficient the *vaidik* could be in things destructive. Here lies the greatness of Brahminism to annihilate anything that questions their social order.

Today, the Muslims are facing a dilemma. The *vaidiks* say they have no objection to co-opt Muslims if they agree to Prophet Mohammed being made an *avatar* and the Allah included among their 330 million gods.

God preaching violence

Inequality is there even in advanced countries but what we have in India is the most gory form of inequality. Mere inequality is not so dangerous as graded inequality. Because this prevents people from becoming angry. To become angry, one must first get disgusted with the graded inequality. The system of graded inequality makes you think that you are destined to be poor and suffering because of the caste you are born. That is why Hindu India cannot see a revolution. If one particular caste revolts, the one above it will immediately crush the revolt. The Brahmin need not come into the picture. In Maharashtra if the Untouchables revolt, the *shudra* caste of Maratha will put them down. The Brahmin need not come.

The Hindus are fond of saying their Hinduism is the only religion in the world that stands for non-violence. But the Hindu's principal god Krishna in his *Bhagawad Gita*, which M.K. Gandhi hailed as his Bible, the god himself preaches war and violence. Krishna offers a philosophical defence of war and killing in the war. The *Gita* also defends the caste system and says the god himself created the caste system. Gandhi being a great defender of the caste system naturally called *Gita* his Bible.

Parashurama kills Kshatriyas

Dr. Ambedkar says without the help of the *Gita* the Brahmin counter-revolution would have died. In the *Gita*, Krishna himself offers philosophical defence of counter-revolution. Krishna tells us not to excite or provoke people to rebellion against the theory of *karma kand*. Krishna tells the Hindus to do their duty as prescribed in the *varna vyavastha*. How can there be any revolution in Hindu India as long as Hindus hold the *Gita* — the gospel of counter-revolution — in great reverence? That is how ever since we became "independent", Hindu India is witnessing a series of counter-revolution one after the other. The Bengali Brahmins, Kayasths and Baidyas (the *Bhadralok*) used marxism as a counter-revolution to crush the Muslims and the Untouchables.

A section of people will crave for revolution and fight for revolution only when they have a strong urge for change. But when you are stuck in a caste, with no hope of promotion or demotion how will the motivation for change come? For example the Kshatriyas, who can be equated to the present-day Thakurs in the cowbelt, were hated and killed by the Brahmins by their Guru Parasurama. The Brahmin-Kshatriya relationship is that of a blood feud. So also the Brahmin-Vaishya relation. Both the Thakurs and Vaishyas hate the Brahmin from the bottom of their heart. Vaishyas are boiling because the Brahmin killed their topmost Vaishya, M.K. Gandhi. But both the Kshatriyas and Vaishyas have been co-opted and made as great defenders of Brahminism. Even when a Brahmin killed Gandhi, the most famous Vaishya, the latter did not rebel against the Brahmins. This is because both the Kshatriyas and Vaishyas did not like their caste status to be disturbed as result of antagonising the Brahmins. The class war between Kshatriyas and Brahmins went on for ages. But the *Manu Smriti* which codified the caste laws and assigned the place for each caste pacified the Kshatriyas and the Vaishyas who have been won over by the Brahmins. Both the Thakurs and Vaishyas are today boiling with anger against the Brahmin but they are not ready to fight fearing they may lose their caste status which has put them in the ruling class and made them effective exploiters.

Religion as a business

Likewise, the Brahmins corrupted and co-opted the *shudras*, even the Backward Castes and adopted many of their gods.

The Brahmins calling their Hindu religion as *Sanatana Dharma* is bullshit. There is nothing *Sanatana* (meaning unchanging) in their religion. They simply abandoned their Vedic gods and started worshipping non-Vedic gods. To the Brahmin, their religion is a matter of trade and commerce. Take the case of the Hindu worshipping the Muslim Sai Baba, a Maharashtra Muslim whom the Muslims despise. If the Muslim Sai Baba brings them business and profit they don't mind embracing him, says Dr. Ambedkar.

Every Hindu must have a caste. He can be a believer, non-believer, atheist, meat-eater or even beef-eater, drunkard or anything. There is no problem. But he has to be a slave of the Brahmin. That is the sole criterion to be a Hindu. The Supreme Court of India itself ruled that Hinduism is not a religion but a way of life.

The gods they created are a wonderful people who have no trace of divinity in them. Dr. Ambedkar in his book, *Riddles in Hinduism* (1987, Maharashtra Govt., *W&S*), says even the topmost god of the Brahmins has been disgraced.

> "Brahma was knocked out of the field of worship on a charge of having committed adultery with his own daughter". (Saraswati). The charge is set out in the *Bhagawat Purana...*" (p.74 Ibid).

Every Brahmin god hates the other Brahmin god. Brahma lost his position to Vishnu. Shiva and Vishnu always fought each other.

A big cock & bull story

So in the process of co-opting and corrupting the non-Hindu original inhabitants, the Brahmins adopted their gods and that is how the total number of Hindu gods and goddesses is put at 330 million. When India became "independent", the country's population was 300 millions but Hindus had 330 million gods — that means more than one god for each citizen of the country. Hinduism is a big cock and bull story. If they declare one god as the most supreme, after sometime this god is dethroned and some other god is installed. The latest supreme god which every Hindu is so much afraid of is Ganesha, the elephant-headed god, who is even today unknown to millions of Hindus in many parts of *Hindustan*.

The Brahmin advice to the people is that they must view their god with fear and reverence (*bhaya-bhakti*). Are the Muslim, Christian, Sikh, Jews afraid of their gods? Where is the need to be afraid of your god when you lead a life of caring and sharing? No child is afraid of the mother. The god is like that mother. Even if the child creates some problem the mother still loves the child. The god should be exactly like that mother. But the Hindu god is not like the mother. That is how the Hindu is damn scared of his god (*bhaya-bakti*).

Hindus have a tribal god Krishna (meaning Black). Krishna is their great sex god and elevated above Shiva. After they manufactured the *Gita*, there is no greater god than Krishna (an OBC of the Yadava caste).

Both Krishna and Rama were mere ordinary men, promoted to godhood. Dr. Ambedkar gives elaborate explanation for Brahmins dethroning some gods and promoting some other. It is all chaotic.

Obedient gods

If the god is supreme for other religionists, to the Hindu his god is a puppet and a servant of the Brahmin. When Indira Gandhi as Prime Minister could not visit the hilltop temple of Tirupati during her election tour, the Tirupati temple priests simply dragged their god down the hill to show it to the PM. A very obedient god.

During the Vedic period the Brahmins ate not only meat but also beef. Their gods were prolific boozers. It is only recently the

Brahmins abandoned meat-eating though the Bengali Brahmins not only eat meat but serve it as *prasad* in their temples. They even adopted a non-Vedic (or pre or non-Aryan Vedic) god Shiva.

The *Tantrik* worship is devoid of any morality which occupies a primary place in all religions. *Tantric* worship is nothing but liquor-guzzling and sexual intercourse (Dr. Ambedkar, p.181, Ibid).

If anybody wants a more elaborate answer to the chaos and confusion in the Hindu religion, one can read the Punjabi Brahmin Arun Shourie's book, *Hinduism, Essence & Consequence.*

Arun Shourie incidentally is the only intellectual the Hindus produced in "independent" India. But even his intellectual sparks died once he joined the Hindu terrorist party (BJP).

Judicial terrorism

Brahmins, through their hundreds of "sacred scriptures"— one contradicting the other —have created a chaotic India. The chaos we see today is the direct result of the clash between the Brahminical (Manu) law and the law of the land as prescribed by the constitution. The failure of democracy is due to the fact that the "Hindu society" as it is today is not at all democratic in form and structure. Caste system breeds corruption, nepotism which forces a Hindu to break the laws formed by the govt. established under democracy. All the constitutional functionaries belong to certain upper castes and they want to favour their castes or amass wealth instead of being fair and just. That is how casteism reigns supreme even in our Supreme Court, Defence Services, Govt. Ministers and all constitutional authorities.

If the Supreme Court judges who are charged with the task of administering justice are themselves casteists and corrupt, how can the justice system succeed? (*Judicial Terrorism*, V.T. Rajshekar & Iqbal Ahmed Shariff, DSA-2006).

First and foremost all constitutional authorities have to be rational, democratic. Then only a democratic govt. can be successful. But every Prime Minister of India favoured his *jati* right from Jawaharlal Nehru. Chief Ministers were downright casteists. The Maharashtra Govt. banned Babasaheb Ambedkar's epoch-making book, *Riddles in Hinduism*, (1987). When the Dalits staged a massive protest they lifted the ban. The Supreme Court favoured the Brahmins when the Tamil Nadu Govt. wanted to open the temple priest (*archaka*) job to non-Brahmins. The Court simply delayed its final judgment on Babri Masjid demolition fearing Hindu wrath.

The Govt., judiciary, media are openly anti-Muslim, anti-Dalit if not ant-human because the value system that governs our ruling class is Brahminical.

Pro-Hindu Supreme Court

Look at our Brahminical marxists of Bengal advocating capitalism, free enterprise and shooting down agitating farmers. They say their defence of the unmarxist actions are not anti-marxist because they were essentially Brahminical and hence nothing wrong in their behaviour. In fact marxism died a natural death when the Brahmin leadership of marxist parties found marxism not antagonistic to their Brahmin values (V.T. Rajshekar, *How Marx Failed in Hindu India?*, DSA-1988).

When the ruling upper castes themselves try to crush and destroy the wishes and aspirations of the oppressed people what can the govt. do? When the govt., judiciary, police, media become upper caste in character, where is the room for justice? Liberty, equality simply died facing the tyrannical Brahminical rule. Take the case of Prime Minister Indira Gandhi sending Army into the Golden Temple and killing hundreds of Sikhs (1984) on the ground that the Sikhs were terrorist. Later Prime Minister P.V. Narasimha Rao simply turned other way when the Hindu terrorists razed to ground Babri Masjid (1992) saying that it was a Hindu temple. And our Hindu Supreme Court refused to intervene in the case in which thousands and thousands of innocent Muslims died.

The Brahminical rulers painted the Muslims as terrorists and the media convinced the reading public defending the Babri Masjid demolition and the Gujarat Genocide of over 2,000 Muslims in 2002. But all lovers of justice know the truth.

What sustains equality and liberty is fellow-feeling (fraternity).

"Without Fraternity, Liberty would destroy equality and equality would destroy liberty. If in democracy liberty does not destroy equality and equality does not destroy liberty, it is because at the basis of both there is fraternity. Fraternity is, therefore, the root of Democracy". (Dr. Ambedkar, *Riddles in Hinduism*, W&S, Vol.4, 1987, Maharashtra Govt., p.283).

God preaching hatred

Is there fraternity in India? How can there be fraternity when one caste hates the other caste? How can the Hindus have fraternity when they are taught their caste does no wrong?

Look at a Brahmin temple. Not even the wife of the *pujari* (priest) can enter the *garbha gudi* (sanctum sanctorum). Each area in the temple is demarcated to certain castes and each caste is proud of the area it is able to occupy in a temple — with the Untouchables kept out yards away.

The temple, therefore, becomes the breeding ground for caste hatred. The very god presiding over this temple preaches hatred.

Gandhi demanded mere entry to *Harijans* into temple — nothing more. But his demand was rejected outright and the *Mahatma* fell silent. Gandhi was simply asked to shut up. And he did.

How can the Brahmins, who call themselves *Bhoodevatas* and hence rulers of the land, produce a new society under such mutual suspicions and hatred between castes and castes? Brahmins know the defects of their Brahminical scriptures and how they come into conflict with equality, liberty and particularly fraternity. They know it but they are not prepared to even admit the defect —let alone discarding their scriptures. Under such circumstances how can democracy succeed in India? We have no hope. Democracy is dead. What we have is the rule of the upper castes.

Sick man of Asia

The gods in all other religions do not uphold inequality, exploitation. But the gods under Brahminical religion themselves propagate and practice inequality and destroy fraternity.

The Brahmin says he is the most merited and knowledgeable person because he is the Brahmin and hence expected to be revered. In other words he is the very representative of the god if not god himself. No. He is above the god.

When such a god on earth takes charge of implementing the provisions of the constitution he will implement as per his conscience. That is how India is reduced to the level of a beggar — the sick man of Asia.

There is none to question the Brahmin. How can India be then called democratic? This is the problem.

Brahminism has contaminated the brain of every child, which grows into adult, with all the filth in their religion; *moksha, punya, papa, karma, swarga*. For each action of the Hindu there is no scientific explanation. But he has a ready Hindu excuse. How can democracy succeed when all the actions of the Hindu are done as per his Hindu belief under which Rama and Krishna, who violate every provision in the constitution of India, are held as divine and commit no mistakes?

Every temple and the Hindu *swami* can be charged with any section under the Indian Penal Code but in Hindu India we have not heard of any temple or *swami* hauled up for their omissions and commissions. Because the Hindu finds nothing wrong in our temples and their godmen. These godmen are more dangerous than the gods. Look at the Shankarachari of Kamakoti — charged with murder, womanising and many other crimes. The fellow is scot free. Merrily going round. Brahmins never found fault with him.

Dr. Ambedkar book burnt

The world's largest red-light district is happily flourishing in the country's biggest city, Bombay, with millions of prostitutes, with at least scores dying daily at a very young age out of disease. Because the Hindu finds nothing wrong in the existence of this flesh trade, in which only the lower caste people are employed. No women's organisation has taken up the cause of these prostitutes because there is not even a single Brahmin prostitute there.

Our Hindu women find nothing wrong with Rama discarding

wife Sita who unable to bear the sorrow finally commits suicide. Why ? Because the Hindu women cannot see reason. They are brainwashed by the myth propagated through the *Ramayana*.

Mothers themselves consent destroying female child in the womb because in Hindu India woman is hated. So much so India is today facing serious shortage of women — a very unhealthy development.

Dr. Ambedkar's two chapters (*Riddle of Rama & Krishna*, appendix 1,) were burnt by the Hindu terrorist party in Bombay and the Maharashtra Govt. banned the book itself because the Hindu found Babasaheb's outbursts un-Hindu.

Why the Hindu did not take Babasaheb criticism of Rama and Krishna as a "scientific inquiry" which may help them to think rationally? Why no Hindu scientist came out in support of Dr. Ambedkar's criticism even when he knows they are true? No. He will not. He is interested in keeping the Brahminical order in tact. Not in science and sanity.

When "thinking" itself is not allowed how can there be rational thinking? That is how "thinking" itself died in India. Even a "rational" Brahmin like Arun Shourie joined the Hindu terrorist party and repudiated all that he wrote against his *jati* when he realised that being a Brahmin he can gain respect, status, wealth and everything else. That is how he ceased to be rational and became a Brahmin first and last — even going to the extent of disowning his own book, *Hinduism, Essence and Consequence* (Vikas, New Delhi, 1979).

India has turned into a vast intellectual desert and this desert is fast expanding because Brahminism has killed our very thinking. When there is no right thinking how can there be right action?

Hindu India will never have a revolution as long as the Brahminical counter-revolution is not crushed. Who is to do it? Brahmins are not interested. Nor will they allow its victims to do it. In the process India is rolling down the precipice and yet the rulers are keeping the country mesmerised in their 9% to 10% GDP clouds. ■
